M000315397

DESCRIPTIVE
PSYCHOLOGY

INTERNATIONAL LIBRARY
OF PHILOSOPHY
Edited by Tim Crane and Jonathan Wolff
University College London

The history of the International Library of Philosophy can be traced back to the 1920s, when C.K. Ogden launched the series with G.E. Moore's *Philosophical Papers* and soon after published Ludwig' Wittgenstein's *Tractus Logico-Philosophicus*. Since its auspicious start, it has published the finest work in philosophy under the successive editorships of A.J. Ayer, Bernard Williams and Ted Honderich. Now jointly edited by Tim Crane and Jonathan Wolff, the I.L.P will continue to publish work at the forefront of philosophical research.

Other titles in the I.L.P. include:

PSYCHOLOGY FROM AN EMPIRICAL STANDPOINT,
SECOND EDITION
With a new introduction by Peter Simons
Franz Brentano

CONTENT AND CONSCIOUSNESS
Daniel C. Dennett

G. E. MOORE: SELECTED WRITINGS
Edited by Thomas Baldwin

A MATERIALIST THEORY OF THE MIND
D. M. Armstrong

DESCRIPTIVE PSYCHOLOGY

Franz Brentano

Translated and edited by
Benito Müller

London and New York

First published 1982
by Felix Meiner Verlag, Hamburg

First published in English 1995
by Routledge
2 Park Square, Milton Park, Abingdon, Oxon, OX14 4RN

Simultaneously published in the USA and Canada
by Routledge
270 Madison Ave, New York NY 10016

Transferred to Digital Printing 2006

English translation © 1995 Benito Müller

Typeset in Times by
Ponting–Green Publishing Services, Chesham, Bucks

All rights reserved. No part of this book may be reprinted
or reproduced or utilized in any form or by any electronic,
mechanical, or other means, now known or hereafter
invented, including photocopying and recording, or in any
information storage or retrieval system, without
permission in writing from the publishers.

British Library Cataloguing in Publication Data
A catalogue record for this book is available from
the British Library.

Library of Congress Cataloging in Publication Data
A catalogue record for this book has been requested
Brentano, Franz Clemens, 1838–1917.
[Deskriptive Psychologie. English]
Descriptive psychology/by Franz Brentano:
translated and edited by Benito Müller.
p.   cm. – (International library of philosophy)
Includes bibliographical references and index.
1. Descriptive psychology.
2. Phenomenological psychology.
I. Müller, Benito, 1958–. II. Title. III. Series.
BF39.8.B7413   1995
150.19'8–dc20   94–44167
CIP

ISBN10: 0–415–10811–X (hbk)
ISBN10: 0–415–40801–6 (pbk)

ISBN13: 978–0–415–10811–9 (hbk)
ISBN13: 978–0–415–40801–1 (pbk)

To Vineeta and Anisha

CONTENTS

ACKNOWLEDGMENTS

I would like to thank Roderick Chisholm and Barry Smith for approaching me with this project, and the Brentano Foundation for having financed it. I am also grateful to Rolf George, Sue Hamilton, Hugh Miller for their helpful comments, and to John Penney for his patience and philological expertise. Last, but certainly not least, I am greatly indebted to Wilhelm Baumgartner for the time he spent with me discussing my suggestions for editorial changes, and for his hospitality in Würzburg.

INTRODUCTION*

I

It would be difficult to exaggerate the influence, direct or indirect, of Franz Brentano's thought upon both philosophy and psychology. Among those he taught himself were Husserl, Meinong, Twardowski, C. Stumpf, A. Marty, Th.G. Masaryk and Freud, and through them Brentano's work influenced Ajdukiewicz, Lukasiewicz, Lesniewski, Kotarbinski, Tarski, Heidegger, Chr.V. Eherenfels, M. Wertheimer, W. Köhler and even Kafka. Yet Brentano's teachings are by no means merely of historical interest. His doctrines of *intentionality* and *evidence* (which did have a strong influence on the moral philosophies of G.F. Stout, Russell and G.E. Moore) remain highly relevant to present-day philosophy of mind, psychology and ethics, and have been taken over and advanced by contemporary thinkers such as R.M. Chisholm.

Brentano and Philosophy[1]

Perhaps the best known fact about Brentano is that he was Husserl's teacher. Yet to think that this exhausts Brentano's philosophical significance is to underestimate Brentano's influence and the importance of his philosophical work in its own right. As concerns, in

---

* Part II of this introduction, which explains and comments on the particular doctrines put forward in Brentano's text, is taken from the German edition: F. Brentano, *Deskriptive Psychologie*, R. Chisholm and W. Baumgartner (eds), Hamburg: Meiner 1982.
1 For a more comprehensive contemporary account of Brentano's life and work see: W. Baumgartner and F.-P. Burkard, 'Franz Brentano; Eine Skizze seines Lebens und seiner Werke', *International Bibliography of Austrian Philosophy*, Amsterdam/Atlanta, GA: Rodopi 1990, pp. 16–53.

particular, the relationship between Brentano and Husserl, Chisholm is much closer to the truth in his choice of 'viewing Husserl as being a student of Brentano rather than viewing Brentano as a teacher of Husserl'.[2] Apart from Brentano's notorious reluctance to publish, one of the reasons for the still prevalent underrating of Brentano's own work might be that he was, unfortunately, only too right in his view of the development of philosophy as following a peculiar law of ascendence and decay.[3] For many of the 'improvements' on Brentano's doctrines suggested by his students and their successors are in fact nothing but inadvertent regressions into the realm of obscurity and even mysticism so vehemently rejected by him. Whether or not Brentano always succeeded in achieving his intended standard of scientific clarity is open to debate. The fact, however, that clarity was one of his main objectives – and, incidentally, the lack thereof one of his criticisms of Husserl[4] – is indisputable. Brentano's explicit rejection of the so-called 'speculative science'[5] proposed by Hegel and Schelling, and his famous fourth habilitation thesis that the method of philosophy is no other than that of natural science (*Vera philosophiae methodus nulla alia nisi scientiae naturalis est*), are testimony to this avowed standard. Indeed, in his methodology Brentano was particularly insistent on a rigorous, ever self-critical analysis of our inner life [*Seelenleben*], of logic and of language. His ambitions were thus, in some ways, very close to those of the so-called positivists;[6] and yet, unlike them, he was by no means ready to abandon metaphysics completely, but only to reject the mysticism and dogmatism of the German Idealists as 'a travesty of genuine metaphysics'.[7] Unfortunately, as Stegmüller rightly laments, this methodology was largely ignored by ontologists or metaphysicians, in particular of the Continental tradition. Instead, they continued to take over everyday language with its vaguenesses

---

2 H. Spiegelberg, *The Context of the Phenomenological Movement*, The Hague: Nijhoff 1981, p.137.
3 See F. Brentano, *Die vier Phasen der Philosophie*, Leipzig: Meiner 1926.
4 See H. Spiegelberg, 'On the Significance of the Correspondence between Brentano and Husserl', in *Grazer Philosophische Studien 5* (1978), pp. 95–116.
5 p. 5.
6 Brentano was indeed favourably impressed by the founder of positivism, A. Comte, on whom he published an article called 'Auguste Comte und die positivistische Philosophie', reprinted in *Die vier Phasen der Philosophie*, pp. 99 ff.
7 H. Spiegelberg, *The Phenomenological Movement*, 2nd ed. Vol. I, The Hague: Nijhoff 1965, p. 33, note 1.

and its misleading grammatical peculiarities, merely to burden it additionally with curious new linguistic constructs.[8]

Given the intellectual honesty of Brentano's methodology, it is not surprising that he came to change some of his positions in the course of his long and fruitful philosophical career, in particular his views on truth and existence. Following Aristotle,[9] the 'early' Brentano was an advocate of a correspondence theory of truth and of the doctrine that the ontologically relevant sense of 'existing' is that of 'being true', and thus he was obliged to accept non-real things, or *irrealia* (see pp. xx–xxii), in his ontology.[10] The first of these views was later rejected in favour of his theory of evidence (mainly developed in his Vienna years) which has been considered by some[11] to be Brentano's most important achievement. As concerns ontology, he later rejected all *irrealia* as linguistic fictions. Indeed, after his 'reistic turn', Brentano saw expressions such as 'existence', 'possibility' and 'necessity' as merely synsemantic in nature, i.e. – like prepositions and conjunctions – as devoid of any descriptive meaning (see pp. xx–xxii).

It is not surprising that some of his early students (especially Meinong and Husserl), having adopted and based their work on some of these early Brentanian doctrines (like that of *irrealia*), felt unable to follow their teacher in his rejection of these.[12] And yet, their indebtedness to Brentano goes beyond merely those of Brentano's early doctrines which he later rejected. Bell's list of Husserl's Brentanian legacy, for example, includes doctrines concerning 'phenomena, intuitions, presentations, judgements, consciousness, intentionality, meaning, language, logic, science, truth, certainty, evidence and analysis', and he rightly points out that only by examining the nature of this legacy can we 'begin to understand elements in Husserl's thought that would otherwise remain either impenetrably obscure or puzzlingly arbitrary and idiosyncratic'.[13] In his list – to

---

8 W. Stegmüller, *Hauptströmungen der Gegenwartsphilosophie*, 3rd ed., Kröner 1965, pp. 39 f.

9 See F. Brentano, *Über die mannigfache Bedeutung des Seienden nach Aristoteles*, Freiburg i.B.: Herder 1862.

10 See F. Mayer-Hillebrand, 'Franz Brentanos Einfluss auf die Philosophie seiner Zeit und der Gegenwart', in *Revue Internationale de Philosophie 78* (1967), pp. 373 f.

11 For example, Mayer-Hillebrand and Stegmüller.

12 In a letter to Bergman of 1 June 1909, Brentano agrees, in general, with Marty's statement that Meinong is 'appropriating the clothes which I [Brentano] have discarded'. [S.H. Bergman, 'Bolzano and Brentano', in *Archiv für Geschichte der Philosophie* 48 (1966), p. 307.]

13 D. Bell, *Husserl*, London: Routledge 1990, p. 4.

which he also adds Brentano's mereological theories (see pp. xvii–xx), extensively discussed in the present lectures and taken over by Husserl into the *Logical Investigations*[14] – Bell mentions the probably best known of Brentano's particular doctrines, namely that of intentionality, which says, very roughly speaking, that psychical acts are always directed toward (intentional) objects. (For a more detailed exposition, see p. xx–xxii).

Although fundamental to Brentano's thought, the doctrines discussed here reflect by no means the full scope of Brentano's interests and teachings. Thus one of the best known applications of his theory of evidence, which so impressed G.E. Moore,[15] was in the field of ethics and is hardly touched in this volume. Finally, 'there is more to Brentano the logician than is usually realised',[16] as Simons puts it in his discussion of Brentano's reform of logic. This reform was based on Brentano's theory of judgment (see pp. xx–xxii), according to which the logical form of simple judgments is that of assertion or denial of existence, rather than the traditional subject-predicate form. 'Detailed presentation of the reform was confined to his lectures on logic, which were continued and modified throughout the period (1874–95) when he was teaching in Vienna'.[17] They influenced in particular Brentano's pupil Twardowski, who, in combining the ideas of Bolzano with Brentano's conception of intentional objects, created a new semantic theory which itself became very influential amongst his students, forming what is now known as the 'Lvov-Warsaw School' of Polish analytic philosophers and logicians (i.e. Ajdukiewicz, Lukasiewicz, Lesniewski and Kotarbinski, who in turn was the teacher of Tarski).[18]

Brentano and Psychology

With his insistence on psychical phenomena having to be described as psychical acts – themselves characterized in terms of being

14 Even though Husserl had left Vienna by the time the present lectures were read by Brentano, he was in possession of a transcript (by Dr Hans Schmidkunz) of the 1887/8 lectures which is kept in the Husserl Archive in Leuven, Holland (call number Q 10).

15 His comment on Brentano's *Vom Ursprung sittlicher Erkenntnis* was that '[i]t would be difficult to exaggerate the importance of this work'. [*International Journal of Ethics* XIX (1903).]

16 P.M. Simons, 'Brentano's Reform of Logic', *Topoi* 6 (1987), pp. 25–38.

17 Simons (1987), p.25.

18 See, for example, J. Wolenski, *Logic and Philosophy in the Lvov-Warsaw School*, Dordrecht: Kluwer 1989.

directed toward intentional objects – and his classification of these psychical acts into presenting, judging and emotive ones, Brentano became the founding father of 'act-psychology', taken up, amongst others, by Meinong, Husserl, Stumpf (another direct pupil of Brentano) and Witasek.[19] Indeed, Brentano was one of the creators of modern psychology, i.e. of psychology as a science, emancipated from philosophy. The year 1874 was very significant for this emancipatory process, for it saw the publication of two fundamental treatises, Brentano's *Psychology from an Empirical Standpoint* (the precursor of the present lectures) and Wundt's *Principles of Physiological Psychology*, each exemplifying paradigmatically one of the two approaches adopted in the course of this emancipation. Wundt, who began his career as a physiologist, became the torch-bearer for the 'experimental' approach pursued, amongst others, by Fechner, Helmholtz and G.E. Müller, a group which 'stood for rigorous experimental technique, descriptive analysis and the importance of learning in perception'.[20] Wundt was furthermore an exponent of content-psychology which, in opposition to act-psychology, sought to base the description of psychical phenomena on the static concept of content. Brentano, in turn, came to be a leading figure of a group, including Hering, Mach (who was corresponding with Brentano[21]) and Stumpf, who 'believed in phenomenological description and nativism in perception'.[22]

Even though for many decades Wundt's treatise had a much stronger influence on the development of experimental psychology than that of Brentano, the debate is by no means closed. Brentano's epistemological considerations, put forward in these lectures, particularly in his discussion of the distinction between genetic and descriptive psychology (see pp. xvii–xx), remain as valid today as when they were first conceived.

Yet Brentano's role in the founding of modern psychology goes beyond his dispute with Wundt. Freud, for example, did study under Brentano between the years 1874 and 1876, and, at his

---

19 Note that 'act-psychology' here is used as a generic term, for many act-psychological systems were put forward, conflicting with each other, in particular as concerns 'Brentano's law' that all psychical phenomena are either presentations or based on presentations.

20 E.G. Boring, *A History of Experimental Psychology*, New York: Appleton-Century-Crofts 1950, pp. 351 f.

21 See J. Thiele, 'Briefe deutscher Philosophen an Ernst Mach', *Synthese* 18 (1968), pp. 285–301.

22 Boring (1950), p. 352.

teacher's instigation, Freud translated the twelfth volume of the *Gesammelte Werke* of Mill[23] in the edition by Th. Gomperz.[24] Even though Brentano rejected the unconscious,[25] it stands to reason not only that Brentano's characterization of the psychical realm had a strong influence on Freud, but also that Freud's belief in active ideas was at least facilitated by Brentano's teachings. R. Wollheim also mentions the 'underlying philosophical assumption that Freud retained throughout his work, and which probably derives from the Viennese philosopher Franz Brentano, [. . .] that every mental state or condition can be analyzed into two components: an idea, which gives the mental state its object or what it is directed upon; and its charge of affect, which gives it its measure of strength or efficacy'.[26]

Last, but not least, Brentano's teachings also had a decisive influence on gestalt psychology, which, in protest against the piecemeal analysis of experience into atomistic elements characteristic of Wundt's school, adopted the view that psychical phenomena must be explained in terms of structured wholes. Brentano's mereological views (see pp. xvii–xx) were taken up and discussed in great detail, amongst others (e.g. Twardowski and Husserl) by Stumpf and Meinong, whose students, Eherenfels, Wertheimer and Köhler, became the founders of the gestalt school.

II

In the foreword to *Vom Ursprung sittlicher Erkenntnis* (1889), Brentano said that the ethical views he set forth there belong to the 'domain of thoughts of a "descriptive psychology" which I now dare to hope to be able to disclose to the public in its full extent in the not too distant future'.[27] Unfortunately, he did not publish a work entitled 'Descriptive Psychology', but many of his writings and dictations on the subject have been published in the various post-

23 Brentano, incidentally, was in correspondence with Mill on logical matters.
24 See Ph. Merlan, 'Brentano and Freud', in *Journal of the History of Ideas* 6 (1945), pp. 375–7, and 10 (1949), p. 451.
25 See, for example, Appendix I in this volume, or *Psychology from an Empirical Standpoint*, London: Routledge & Kegan Paul 1973, pp. 54 ff. (in particular 57–8) and 101–37.
26 R. Wollheim, *Sigmund Freud*, New York: Viking Press 1971, pp. 20 f.
27 F. Brentano, *Vom Ursprung sittlicher Erkenntnis*, 3rd ed., Oskar Kraus (ed.), Hamburg: Meiner, 1969, p.3.

humous works in the *Philosophische Bibliothek*.[28] And he gave several courses of lectures on the subject at the University of Vienna. Three different lecture manuscripts have been preserved.

The first of these was given in 1887–8 and was entitled *Deskriptive Psychologie*. The second, entitled *Deskriptive Psychologie oder beschreibende Phänomenologie* was given in 1888–9. (Although the term '*Phänomenologie*' occurred in the title, it does not seem to have been used in the lectures themselves.) The third, entitled simply *Psychognosie*, was given in 1890–1. The main text of the present book is taken from the lecture of 1890–1.

The following material is added in the appendices: (1) the description of 'inner perception' from the lectures of 1887–8; (2) the general account of 'descriptive psychology' from the lectures of 1888–9; (3) 'Of the Content of Experiences' from the lectures of 1887–8; (4) 'Psychognostic Sketch I', from 1901; (5) 'Psychognostic Sketch II', also from 1901; and (6) an undated manuscript from the same general period entitled 'Perceiving and Apperceiving'.[29]

The Parts of Human Consciousness

The lectures of 1887–8 and those of 1888–9 were concerned for the most part with problems of the psychology of the senses. But the lectures of 1890–1, which constitute our main text, are concerned with the nature of descriptive psychology as such and with the formulation of a doctrine of psychological categories.

In 1895, Brentano published the following statement about the nature of descriptive psychology:

---

28 See, in particular, Volume II of the second edition of the *Psychologie vom empirischen Standpunkt, Von der Klassifikation der psychischen Phänomene*, Leipzig: 1874, 2nd ed. O. Kraus (ed.), Hamburg: Meiner 1925 (unaltered reprint Hamburg: Meiner 1971), [Engl. tr.: *Psychology from an Empirical Standpoint, The Classification of Mental Phenomena*, L. McAlister (ed.), London: Routledge & Kegan Paul 1973, pp. 271–311]; Volume 3 of the *Psychologie, Vom sinnlichen und noetischen Bewusstsein*, O. Kraus (ed.), Leipzig: Meiner 1928, (2nd ed. Hamburg: Meiner 1968 (unaltered reprint with new introduction by F. Mayer-Hillebrand, Hamburg: Meiner 1974) [Engl. tr.: *Sensory and Noetic Consciousness*, L. McAlister (tr.), London: Routledge & Kegan Paul 1981]; *Grundzüge der Ästhetik*, F. Mayer-Hillebrand (ed.), Hamburg: Meiner 1959; *Untersuchungen zur Sinnespsychologie*, 2nd ed. Roderick M. Chisholm and Reinhard Fabian (eds), Hamburg: Meiner 1979.

29 Appendix 6, which is listed in Brentano's Nachlass as Ps 29, is there entitled: '*Perzipieren, Apperzipieren, deutlich Apperzipieren, kopulativ Apperzipieren, transcendendent Apperzipieren*'.

My school distinguishes a *psychognosy* and a *genetic psychology* (in distant analogy to geognosy and geology). The one shows all the final psychical constituents from the combination of which arises the totality of psychical phenomena, in the same way as the totality of words arises from letters. Its implementation could serve as basis for a *characteristica universalis* as envisaged by Leibniz and, before him, Descartes. The other one teaches us about the laws according to which phenomena come and disappear. Given that, due to the undeniable dependency of the psychical functions on the processes in the nervous system, the conditions are to a large extent physiological, one can see here how psychological investigations must intertwine with physiological ones. It might more likely be suspected that psychognosy could completely disregard anything physiological and thus dispense with all instrumental auxiliary means. Yet already the mentioned analysis of experiences, be it in the domain of hearing, be it in the domain of vision or even in the one of the primitive sensory phenomena (a domain where it has thus far been carried out with extreme imperfection), can only achieve its most essential successes by means of cleverly conceived instrumental auxiliary means; and this [sort of] work is psychognostic.[30]

What are the ultimate psychical constituents of consciousness? Brentano's use of such terms as 'part' ['*Teil*'] and 'element' ['*Element*'] may appear somewhat strange to contemporary philosophers. For he does not hesitate to say that psychical acts are *parts* of human consciousness. How could an act of thinking be a 'part' of consciousness?

It is essential to keep in mind that, according to Brentano, predicates ('red' ['*rot*']) can always be replaced by concrete terms ('a red-thing' ['*ein Rotes*']). Instead of saying 'A rose is red', we may say 'A rose is a red-thing'. The first statement may seem to relate a rose to an abstract object which is a property (as in 'A rose exemplifies redness'). But the second statement would seem to relate two *things* – a rose and a red-thing. What, then, is the relation between the two things? Brentano explicates it by reference to part and whole. He says that, if we can correctly say of a rose that it is a red thing, then a rose and a red-thing are both parts of the same thing.

30 *Meine letzten Wünsche für Österreich*, Stuttgart: Cotta 1895, pp. 84 f.

Again, if we say of a person that he sees, we may reformulate this by saying 'A person is a seeing-thing [*ein Sehender*]'. In this case, too, we are relating concrete things. And once again, according to Brentano, we are dealing with the part-whole relation. 'A person is a seeing-thing', according to Brentano's final view, tells us not that a person and a seeing-thing are parts of the same thing, but that a person is a part of a seeing-thing. The person – or the self – is an ultimate unified substance [*eine letzte einheitliche Substanz*] which may be a part of that accident which is a seeing-thing. But the self has *no* parts. Hence the parts of consciousness must not be identified with the parts of the self or the soul.

Brentano distinguishes two different types of parts – those which are separable [*ablösbar*] and merely distinctional ones [*bloss distinktionelle*]. Normally, we think of parts as exemplifying actual separability (or detachability [*Abtrennbarkeit*]). Actual separability is illustrated by the parts of a physical thing. One may distinguish, say, the left and right halves of a table-top: they can be separated from each other and either can exist without the other. Separable parts are exemplified in consciousness by seeing and hearing, or by remembering and desiring: consciousness may continue after one ceases to see or to hear or to remember or to desire. Brentano puts this fact by saying that the thinking-thing [*der Denkende*] may continue to exist after any of these parts is separated from it.

Brentano also distinguishes between mutual [*gegenseitige*] and one-sided separability. This distinction is of fundamental importance to his theory of the self and his theory of substance. Consider a person who is both seeing and hearing. The seeing and the hearing are related by mutual separability: either is such that the one may continue after the other ceases to be. In this respect the seeing and the hearing – the seeing-thing and the hearing-thing – are like the two halves of the table-top: either half may continue to exist after the other is destroyed.

One-sided separability is illustrated by the relation of the thinker to the see-er. It is also illustrated by the relation between experiencing [*Empfinden*] and noticing [*Bemerken*], and by the relation between presenting [*Vorstellen*] and desiring [*Begehren*]. The first member of each pair can exist without the second, but the second cannot exist without the first. Brentano says that *psychical acts* may be identified with the separable parts of consciousness. He notes that we can also speak 'in a certain sense' of another kind of part – these are *merely distinctional*. Such parts, one could say, are distinguishable in thought but not in reality. An example is provided by what he calls 'mutually pervading parts' [*sich durchwohnende Teile*]. The objects of sensation provide us with examples of such parts. Thus spatial determination [*Räumlichkeit*] and quality are pervading parts of the primary objects of experience. Examples of such pervading parts are also provided by the act of judgment expressed by 'There is a truth'. The pervading parts of this act of judgment are its affirmative quality, its being directed [*Gerichtetsein*] at the object truth, its evidence, and its apodeictic modality. Brentano also uses the term '*concrescente Teile*' for pervading parts. He observes that 'a commonly accepted scientific term is missing'.[31] Possibly 'inner nature' or 'integral part' could be used for 'pervading part'.

Let us now consider the general conception of consciousness that Brentano had accepted in 1890–1.

The Intentional Relation

Every psychical act is *intentional* in that it is directed upon an object. The doctrine of intentionality that is set forth in the present lectures is essentially that of the first edition of the *Psychology from an Empirical Standpoint* (1874). The intentional object is always 'immanent'; it is something that is non-real, or insubstantial [*unwesenhaft*], but it may be said to exist – and to exist in itself – to the extent that the thinker *has* it as his intentional object. It is a non-real correlate of the thinking that has it as its object.

The intention thus involves as relation a pair of correlates of which 'the one alone is real, [whereas] the other is not something real [*nichts Reales*]'.[32] The following are examples of such pairs: seeing and what is seen; presenting and what is presented; loving and what is loved; willing and what is willed; denying and what is denied. Brentano observes:

> A person who is being thought [*ein gedachter Mensch*] is as little something real as a person who has ceased to be [*gewesener Mensch*]. The person who is being thought hence has no proper cause and cannot properly have an effect. But when the act of consciousness (the thinking of the person)

31 p. 22.
32 p. 24.

is effected, the person who is being thought (the non-real correlate of the person) coexists [*ist mit da*].[33]

Brentano was later to reject this doctrine of intentional inexistence,[34] or mental holding [*geistiges Inhaben*[35]]. According to his final view, the statement 'There is something which is being thought [*ein Gedachtes*]' is an improper formulation of 'There is a thinking-thing [*ein Denkendes*]'; statements ostensibly about immanent objects are actually statements only about the thinker who may be said to have those objects. According to this final view, there are no insubstantial entities; everything is an *ens reale*.[36]

Brentano divides intentional phenomena into: presenting; judging; and emotive phenomena (or loving and hating).

Every psychical act involves the *presentation* of an object. The objects of presentations are normally restricted to individual things or *entia realia* (e.g. to such things as horses, trees, unicorns). In Brentano's later writings, he contends that the objects of presentations can *only* be individual things or *entia realia*: what we think of is always an individual thing, or *concretum*, as qualified in some way or other. But in the present lectures, Brentano holds that certain non-things [*Undinge*] (for example, truth as well as certain immanent objects) may be objects of presenting.

Judgment is a matter of accepting or rejecting an object of a presentation. Judging is a 'superposed' ['*supraponierter*'] psychical act since it necessarily presupposes another psychical act – that of presenting. Since every judgment is either an acceptance or a rejection, judgments are always either affirmative or negative. And since the object of a judgment is the same as the object of the presentation that underlies the judgment, the object of judgment may be an individual thing or *ens reale*. The object of judgment, therefore, need not be the kind of propositional entity designated by means of such expressions as 'that there are horses' or 'that there are no dragons'. For example, if a person believes that there are horses, then *horse* constitutes the object of an affirmative judgment; the object is not a non-thing designated by some such phrase as 'the

---

33 p. 24. Concerning the notion of '*gedachter Mensch*' see also note 8a at the end of this volume.

34 Note that Brentano's term 'inexistence' derives from 'to exist in' and is not to be confused with 'non-existence'.

35 See, for example, p. 155.

36 See *Wahrheit und Evidenz*, Hamburg: Meiner 1974; and *Die Abkehr vom Nichtrealen*, Hamburg: Meiner 1966.

being of horses' or 'that there are horses'. And if the person believes that there are no dragons, then *dragon* constitutes the object of a negative judgment; the object is not a non-thing designated by some such phrase as 'the non-being of dragons' or 'that there are no dragons'.

There are different *modes* of judgment. In particular, one may distinguish judgments that are assertoric from judgments that are apodeictic. For example, if a person can be said to judge that round squares are impossible, then he apodeictically rejects round squares. And we may distinguish judgments that are evident from those that are non-evident or 'blind'.

Brentano assumes that there are two dimensions of *emotion* – which he calls 'loving' and 'hating' respectively. (Other possible pairs of terms are 'pro-emotion' and 'anti-emotion'; and 'positive interest' and 'negative interest'.) Emotive phenomena are thus like judgment in being either positive or negative. And they are like judgment in presupposing presentations: the object of any given emotion is the object of the corresponding presentation. Loving and hating are therefore like judgment in being superposed acts, for they are necessarily such that they presuppose another act.

Every act of thinking, according to Brentano, has itself as a 'secondary object'. If I think of a mountain, then the mountain is the 'primary object' of my thinking; and my thinking of a mountain is the 'secondary object' of my thinking. Brentano also puts the latter point by saying that my thinking of a mountain is an object of my 'inner perception'. He writes: 'The fact that there is no consciousness without any intentional relation at all is as certain as the fact that, apart from the object upon which it is primarily directed, consciousness, on the side, has itself as an object'.[37] He cites this example: 'The experiencing of the colour and the concomitant experiencing of this experiencing are directed towards [*gehen auf*] different objects'.[38]

Every assertoric judgment that is evident has as its object something that is an object of inner perception or of secondary consciousness. And every object of inner perception can be an object of an evident judgment. If I am thinking about a mountain, then I can judge with evidence – and therefore with truth – that I am thinking about a mountain.

37   p. 26.
38   p. 27.

Sensation

Sensations are fundamental psychical acts. They are, therefore, unlike those 'superposed acts', such as judging, which presuppose psychical acts other than themselves. They are those acts 'which have sensory phenomena as primary objects. That is to say, they contain as primary relation a presenting of concrete sensory content'.[39] But the act of sensation is not *merely* a *presentation*: it is also judgmental, for it involves an instinctive and 'blind' acceptance of the object. And it is often emotive – involving a love or hate of the object.

The *objects* of sensation are individual things. 'That which we experience is a *concretum*, a qualitatively and spatially specified unity which is only individual through the union of these specifications'.[40]

According to the view of the present lectures, those individual things which are the objects of sensation are intentional objects. They exist as insubstantial correlates of experience. Experiencing is something real; the object of experiencing is something non-real. But according to Brentano's later, reistic view of intentionality, there is nothing that is insubstantial. Hence Brentano's final view is that the individual things which are the objects of sensation do not exist. (The object of his fears is a certain individual. But this individual does not exist.[41]) From the fact that I sense a red patch, it will follow that it is evident to me that I sense a red patch, but it will not follow that the red patch exists.

Brentano sometimes calls sensation 'external perception' in order to contrast it with inner perception. One should note that this is not the contemporary philosophical use of 'perception'. Thus Brentano uses 'see' and 'hear', respectively, to refer to the sensing of a visual content and to the sensing of an auditory content. Hence, given his final view about the existence of sensory content, he can say that, from the fact that I *see* a patch of colour or *hear* a certain note, it does not follow that the patch of colour or the note *exists*.

Every sense-object has both spatial and qualitative determinations. Brentano also puts this point by saying that every sense-object

39 p. 91.
40 *Untersuchungen zur Sinnespsychologie*, 2nd ed., p. 167.
41 See Brentano's letter to A. Marty in his *The True and the Evident*, R. Chisholm (ed.), London: Routledge & Kegan Paul, 1966, p. 77, or the Appendices XIII and XIV (pp. 315 ff.) in his *Psychology from an Empirical Standpoint*.

involves a *sensible quality* that fills a *sensible space*. With respect to the presentation of spatial features, then, Brentano is a 'nativist' and not an 'empiricist'. He discussed the issues between nativism and empiricism in much greater detail in his 1888–9 lectures on Descriptive Psychology.[42]

The distinction between *colouredness* [*Kolorit*] and *non-coloured-ness* [*Nicht-Kolorit*] is illustrated in the visual sense by the distinction between chromatic and non-chromatic colours. There are, according to Brentano, three simple or elementary chromatic colours (red, blue and yellow) and two simple or elementary non-chromatic colours (black and white). All other colours are compounds of elementary colours. Brentano describes the nature of the relevant compounding in terms of the nature of sensible space. Analogous considerations hold of the other senses. Thus, in the case of hearing, *colouredness* is exhibited in pitch. And in the case of the other senses, it is exhibited in flavour and odour.

The second component [*Moment*] of quality is the distinction between *lightness* [*Helligkeit*] and *darkness* [*Dunkelheit*]. Unlike other psychologists of sensation, Brentano does not restrict this distinction to the visual sense. It has an analogue for the sense of hearing (compare the distinction between *high* and *low*). And, according to Brentano, it has one further analogue which enables us to unite the so-called 'lower' senses into a single third sense.

Proteraesthesis

Are *temporal* dimensions presented in a way that is analogous to the presentation of spatial dimensions? This question takes us to Brentano's doctrine of 'proteraesthesis, or original association'. In his 1887–8 lectures, he introduced his discussion of this doctrine with the following remarks:

> When I spoke of the content of experience, you presumably all understood, more or less, what I meant: now, that I speak of original association I must fear that none of my audience knows what I am actually aiming at. Indeed, the expression does not appear in any manual or textbook of psychology. And, it seems to me that the fact to which it refers is itself not apprehended

42 His views are very similar to those of C. Stumpf, in *Über den psychologischen Ursprung der Raumvorstellung*, Leipzig: 1873.

and interpreted in anything I have seen. I myself have never published anything about it, which is why the doctrine is [only] taught orally from certain chairs held by students of mine.

The source of our concept of time, according to Brentano, is this experience of proteraesthesis or original association. But it is a phenomenon that accompanies every sensation. Examples are the hearing of a melody, the seeing of something in motion and the seeing of something at rest. In each case, we experience a succession [ein Nacheinander]: in the first case one note preceding another note; in the second case the moving object being now in one place and now in another; and in the third case one and the same thing remaining exactly where it was.

The experience of any such succession involves what might be called, somewhat misleadingly, an experience of the past [Vergangenheitsempfindung]. The duration of such a proteraesthesis is very brief. For example, in a single experience we 'see' part of the circular motion of the second-hand of a clock, but we do not see the entire circular motion, and if the motion were not sufficiently swift we would not see it at all. Yet, brief as such experiences are, they enable us to acquire the concepts of past, present and future, the concepts of before and after, and the concept of a temporal continuum extending indefinitely in two directions.

Thus Brentano writes in the present lectures: 'The intuitive timespan of proterosis[43] contains the relation of earlier and later. Everything else, including the future, arises from this in an unintuitive manner.'[44] But the intuitive determinations are '[. . .] sufficient in serving to form unintuitive presentations [. . .]'.[45]

Consider the proteraesthesis involved in the hearing of the first notes of a melody – say a, b, c and d.

Some have said that the field of consciousness is temporally extended in the way in which, say, the visual field may be said to be spatially extended. According to this view, just as a red spot can be at the left side of the visual field and a blue spot at the right, so, too, the note c can be in the present part of the sensory field while b is

---

43 Concerning the relationship of the concepts of proterosis and proteraesthesis see pp. 91f., 94f., 98, 100f., 101–3, and also B. Müller, 'Proterosis, Proteraesthesis and Noticing a Red Tint', in Brentano Studien, forthcoming.

44 p. 106.

45 p. 106.

in a part that is past and *a* is in a part that is even more past. But does it make sense to say of the note *b* that it is past? If *b* is no longer in the present, we cannot say that it *is* in a part that is past. If we take tense seriously, as Brentano does, we cannot say of the field of consciousness or of the objects of sensation that they (now) *have* a temporal extension.[46]

We may say of the earlier notes in the experience of proteraesthesis that they are 'presented as being past'.[47] At the time of the hearing of *d*, the note *c* is presented as being past, the note *a* is presented as being even more past than *b*. Yet nothing *has* the attribute of being past. If anything *has* a given attribute, then that thing exists now and cannot be said merely to exist in the past. How, then, are we using the word 'past' when we say that the note is presented as past?

Brentano speaks of that peculiar modification through which what presented itself earlier as being present is seen and judged to be past.[48] In other words, the adjective 'past' should not be thought of as expressing a genuine attribute at all. Rather, it may express what Brentano called 'a modifying attribute'. What, then, is a modifying attribute?

If we say of something that it is an 'apparent king' or a 'supposed king', we do not imply that the thing *is* a king and our adjectives, therefore, are only 'modifying'.[49] Other adjectives that may thus be modifying are: 'deposed', 'departed', 'so-called', 'former', 'apparent'. Such adjectives *subtract from* what is suggested by the noun 'king'. It is clear that 'past' functions as such a modifying adjective. If we say of someone that he is 'a past king', we do not imply that he *is* a king. 'A past N is not an N. It is modified.'[50]

According to the view of the present lectures, then, the adjective

---

46 But everything is temporal in that everything is such that either it did exist or it will exist. Brentano puts this point by saying that everything exists as a temporal boundary.

47 See pp. 102–4, and also Brentano's *Philosophical Investigations on Space, Time and the Continuum*, Barry Smith (tr.), London: Croom Helm, 1988, p. 79, or pp. 326 ff. (Appendix XIV) and pp. 330 ff. (Appendix XV) in his *Psychology from an Empirical Standpoint*.

48 See p. 103, and also Brentano's *Philosophical Investigations on Space, Time and the Continuum*, p. 71.

49 Compare Volume III of the *Psychologie: Vom sinnlichen und noetischen Bewusstsein*, p. 46. There is a detailed study of such modifying adjectives in Marty's posthumous '*Von den logisch nicht begründeten synsemantischen Zeichen*', published in Otto Funke, *Grundfragen zur Bedeutungslehre*, Leipzig: Reisland 1928; this work originally appeared in *English Studies* 62 and 63 (1928).

50 p. 100.

'past' serves to modify its subject in this way. '"Past" is to "tone" not like a determining enriching, but like a modifying determination. Tone is contained in past tone not properly but modifyingly [. . .].'[51] When the subjects of our example have a sensation which has as *its* primary object the note *b*, they also experience a proteraesthesis which has as its primary object – *not* the past note *a* – but the past sensation of *a*. Thus, where the *secondary* object of the sensation is a present sensation, the *primary* object of the proteraesthesis is a past sensation. This means that the primary object of the proteraesthesis is a *modified intentional relation* – an intentional relation that is past. The modifying attribute of pastness was thought to be quantitative and capable of degrees.

Brentano was subsequently to reject this view, according to which proteraesthesis always involves a modifying attribute, and to replace it by a conception of temporal modes of consciousness.[52] But he continued to hold that sensation and proteraesthesis are inseparable.

<table>
<tr><td>Kirchberg am Wechsel</td><td align="right">*Roderick M. Chisholm*</td></tr>
<tr><td>1 September 1981</td><td align="right">*Brown University*</td></tr>
</table>

Wilhelm Baumgartner
Universität Würzburg

Oxford   *Benito Müller*
1 June 1993   *Wolfson College, Oxford*

---

51 See Brentano's *Psychologie vom empirischen Standpunkt*, Vol. III, pp. 44 ff.
52 The later conception is summarized in the editors' notes to the present work; see, in particular, note 6, p. 175. In Edmund Husserl, *Zur Phänomenologie des inneren Zeitbewusstseins*, The Hague: Nijhoff, 1966, there is a criticism of Brentano's early views about our consciousness of time (cf. pp. 10–18). Husserl does not mention Brentano's subsequent view that our consciousness of time has its source in modes of presentation. See Oskar Kraus, 'Zur Phänomenognosie des Zeitbewusstseins', *Archiv für die gesamte Psychologie*, Vol. 75 (1930), pp. 1–22. Kraus's paper was occasioned by the publication of Martin Heidegger's edition of Husserl's '*Vorlesung zur Phänomenologie des inneren Zeitbewusstseins*,' in Husserl's *Jahrbuch für Philosophie und phänomenologische Forschung*, Vol. IX (1928), pp. 367–489. Brentano's lectures had been the impetus for Husserl's work on this topic, as Husserl notes; see E. Husserl, *Gesammelte Werke – Husserliana*, Vol. X, The Hague: Nijhoff, 1966, p. xv.

Part I

THE TASK OF PSYCHOGNOSY

1

PSYCHOGNOSY AND GENETIC PSYCHOLOGY*

1. Psychology is the science of people's inner life [*Seelenleben*], that is, the part of life which is captured in inner perception [*innere Wahrnehmung*]. It aims at exhaustively determining (if possible) the elements of human consciousness and the ways in which they are connected, and at describing the causal conditions which the particular phenomena are subjected to.

The first is the subject matter of psychognosy, the second that of genetic psychology.

2. The difference between the two disciplines is fundamental. It manifests itself, in particular, in two essential relationships:
(a) Psychognosy, one could say, is pure psychology, whereas it would not be inappropriate to refer to genetic psychology as physiological psychology.
(b) The former is an exact science, whereas the latter will presumably have to renounce forever any claim to exactness.
Both [of these points] can be set forth in a few words.

3. I am saying that only psychognosy is to be called pure psychology.

The meaning and the correctness of this [statement] may be shown by the following brief reflection.

4. The occurrence of both human consciousness and its different phenomena is, according to experience, tied to certain physiological events, which we have learnt to understand as physico-chemical

---

* The following notation has been adopted: '|' and '#' are used to indicate the pagination and the footnotes of the German edition, respectively; while '*' is used for the footnotes new to this edition.

3

processes. If, according to what we said, it is the concern of genetic psychology to acquaint us with the conditions under which specific phenomena occur, then it is evident that genetic psychology will 1|2 never be able to achieve its task fully and properly ¦ without mentioning physico-chemical processes and without reference to anatomical structures.

5. Psychognosy is different. It teaches nothing about the causes that give rise to human consciousness and which are responsible for the fact that a specific phenomenon does occur now, or does not occur now or disappears. Its aim is nothing other than to provide us with a general conception of the entire realm of human consciousness. It does this by listing fully the basic components out of which everything internally perceived by humans is composed, and by enumerating the ways in which these components can be connected. Psychognosy will therefore, even in its highest state of perfection, never mention a physico-chemical process in any of its doctrines [*Lehrsatz*].

For, correct as it is to say that such processes are preconditions for consciousness, one must resolutely contradict the person who, out of a confusion of thought, claims that our consciousness in itself is to be seen as a physico-chemical event, that it itself is composed out of chemical elements.

6. Chemical elements are substances [*Stoffe*] which, by themselves, are unintuitive [*unanschaulich*], and which can only be characterized in relative terms by considering manifold direct and indirect effects on our consciousness. The elements of inner life, i.e. the different most simple constituents, by contrast, are without exception intuitively contained in our consciousness.

In enumerating them, psychognosy can therefore leave out any reference to the physiological, the physico-chemical realm.

7. And the same evidently applies to the ways of connecting the elements of consciousness. These connections are as alien to those mentioned in chemistry, as the elements of consciousness are to chemical items.

8. Psychognosy is in this sense pure psychology and as such 2|3 essentially different from genetic psychology. ¦

9. I have emphasized yet another important difference. I claimed that

4

psychognosy is an exact science, and that, in contrast, genetic psychology, in all its determinations, is an inexact one.

10. What do I mean by this? What is to be understood by an exact science, as opposed to an inexact one?

11. There has sometimes been talk of exact science as opposed to a so-called speculative science. The latter name was used, in particular, to honour the bold constructs of certain men, who admired a recent past as a marvel of philosophical genius.

I would be gravely misunderstood if, in our case, one were to think of this distinction.

No, this expression 'speculative science' is a gross misuse of the term science. A SCHELLINGian or HEGELian system is bare and void of all scientific character.

12. My distinction is completely different. There are sciences which can formulate their doctrines sharply and precisely. Others are forced to content themselves with undetermined and vague formulae. A mathematician doesn't say: the sum of the angles of a triangle is often, or usually, equal to two right angles. But he says that this is always and without exception the case.

Likewise, in mechanics, the law of inertia and so many other postulates and doctrines are formulated in a sharp and exact manner.

In contrast, we have, e.g., meteorology, even if it is only concerned with very simple things like the relative temperature of a summer or a winter month. 'Often', 'mostly', 'on average' are expressions which must be used to weaken the precision of meteorological claims, in order for them to be true. Meteorology is not capable of determining fully and taking into account the factors influencing meteorological events. Meteorological results thus often vary within wide margins.

13. My intention was to point out the similarity of this case to that of genetic psychology, insofar as ¦ it is disadvantaged compared to psychognosis.

14. [This is so] because the doctrines of psychognosy are sharp and precise. They might still show some gaps here and there – after all, the same holds in the case of mathematics. Doubts about their correctness might still arise here and there – and certainly we will

5

often be tempted by incorrect views, and will sometimes hear important researchers contradict (fight) each other in their claims. Nevertheless, psychognostic doctrines do allow and [indeed] do demand a precise formulation:

like, e.g., that the phenomenon of violet = red-blue, even though quite a few people may be undecided whether to follow BRÜCKE or HERING in this case.

15. Genetic psychology is different. The laws of Becoming [*Gesetze des Werdens*] which it postulates are not strictly valid. They are subject to a more or less frequent occurrence of exceptions. Like meteorology, genetic psychology needs to diminish the precision of all its doctrines, by using terms like 'often' and 'mostly', in order for them to be true.[1]

16. The same character can also quite clearly be attributed to the laws of psychical Becoming which have been formulated without giving the physiological preconditions, like, e.g., certain so-called laws of association of ideas [*Ideenassoziation*], which were already used in mnemonics in antiquity.

17. Some have talked, in this context, of a law of similarity and again of a law of continuity, according to which one thought revives [*wieder erwecken*] another. This happens very often, but in other cases it doesn't, and where it happens, it does so in such manifold different ways that no determined prediction can be based upon them. (Joh. MÜLLER[2] says that the laws themselves contradict each other.) The reason for this is that the most immediate preconditions for the return of thoughts are not, or, in any case, not exhaustively, identified in these laws.

18. More hopeful, with respect to full exactness, are those claims of genetic psychology in which physiological preconditions are given. But unfortunately we are presently, and presumably always will be, incapable of determining the immediate physiological antecedents of 4!5 a psychical event, ¦ let alone determining them in an exhaustive manner. The lack of exactness will thus inevitably continue to exist.

Example: Stimulation of a retinal part by a light-ray of a certain frequency induces the phenomenon of blue. But this [is] not always [so], as it is not true in case of

6

(a) colour-blindness,
(b) interruption of the conductor, severance of the nerve,
(c) losing in competition [*Besiegtwerden im Wettstreit*],
(d) replacement by a hallucination.

(And who could claim that there are no other disturbances which bring about exceptions by creating an anomaly in the most immediate physiological preconditions, given that our examples make use only of the more distant of these preconditions.)

19. The necessary inexactness of genetic psychology could likewise be demonstrated by using any other doctrines which it puts forward.

20. To conclude, you now understand sufficiently the two differences, which – as I said – give an essentially different character to the doctrines of psychognosy and to those of genetic psychology,

(a) insofar as the one is pure psychology, and the other psychophysical,
(b) insofar as the claims of the one are exact, while those of the other [are not, and] presumably never will acquire the character of exactness.

21. We have thus divided psychology into psychognosy and genetic psychology. And we have clarified the meaning of this separation by pointing at two essential differences between these disciplines:

(a) Psychognosy is pure psychology, while genetic psychology is physiological psychology.
(b) Psychognosy belongs to the exact sciences, while genetic psychology is, and presumably will remain forever, incapable of formulating its doctrines other than in the imprecise manner of the inexact sciences.

At the same time I vehemently rejected the misguided view that,
5!6 in saying this, my intention was to discredit the scientific ! legitimacy of genetic psychology or to describe it as a hotbed of arbitrary speculations.

22. The division of the two disciplines will also be beneficial to the progress of psychological research, particularly if their natural order

7

becomes clear. After all, division and ordering of difficulties is a crucial precondition to their resolution.

When DESCARTES first embarked on his brilliant career, he became engrossed in serious contemplation about the Method. The results of these he put down in the *Discours de la méthode*.

In this, four fundamental rules for research are put forward. Two of them have no other purpose than to recommend [on the one hand] the necessary division of difficulties and [on the other] that the individual difficulties are to be dealt with in an order which is fixed and, as far as possible, outlined by nature.

Instead of dividing psychognostic questions from questions pertaining to genetic psychology, psychologists, up to the present day, usually mix these questions in manifold ways. In doing so, they decidedly contravene DESCARTES' rules. And this grave contravention of the Method presumably contributed decisively to slowing down, or indeed completely frustrating, progress in psychology.

Having divided the disciplines, it will be clear without much reflection what their natural order is. Psychognosy is prior in the natural order.

In the same way as orognosy and geognosy* precede geology in the field of mineralogy, and anatomy generally precedes physiology in the more closely related field of the human organism, psychognosy, according to what has been determined so far, must be positioned prior to genetic psychology.

23. All the same, this is not to say that psychogenetic knowledge could not become useful at some point in psychognostic research.

On the contrary, one will very often be able to draw support from such knowledge. But then there is no pair of sciences between which there are no reciprocal services. Let us look, e.g., at the realm of the senses.

(a) The arousal [*Erweckung*] of sensory phenomena, which are to be studied, happens according to the laws of genetic psychology. What an impediment to the psychognosy of the senses it would be, if the psychognost did not use them [the laws of genetic psychology] to call up the sensation to be analysed.

---

* In the O.E.D. we find 'geognosy', 'geognostic', and 'geognost'. Hence I shall use 'psychognosy', 'psychognostic', and 'psychognost' as translations for '*Psychognosie*', '*psychognostisch*' and '*Psychognost*', respectively.

(b) And he will use these laws not only for the arousal, but also to retain the phenomenon, for otherwise it would pass too fleetingly for a careful observation and a trustworthy analysis.

(c) Still more! In order to notice certain peculiar characteristics of a phenomenon, it is very important to compare it to other phenomena that are in certain ways similar, in other ways dissimilar to it. Hence one must try to present to oneself such phenomena together with each other or in rapid succession. One must let these phenomena vary by experimenting psychognostically. It is evident that in doing so, knowledge of genetic psychology is used to a greater or lesser extent.

(d) In many cases, psychognosy can also make use of the findings of genetic psychology in the way in which they were used, e.g., by HELMHOLTZ[3] in his investigations on the nature of tone colours. (Namely the use of resonators, tuned to specific tones: the resonators enabled one to distinguish these tones in sounds in which they did not clearly stand out). In following this experiment, one could admittedly still doubt whether the tone-phenomenon in question really contained the overtones, or whether it is to be regarded only as the effect of the simultaneous influence of different soundwaves, each of which would separately have brought about one of those tones. But, in sharply concentrating his attention, HELMHOLTZ later succeeded in really hearing the tones which he could only suppose to exist in the sound. The genetic experiment gave rise to the right hypothesis, and this was in this case, as so often, essential in facilitating the discovery of the truth. ¦

(e) in vowels.[4]

(f) The production of simple tastes and smells is essential for the classification of such an unclear domain. If there is hope for such a classification, then it is only by using genetic laws.

(g) There is yet another way in which knowledge of the statements of genetic psychology may become widely useful in the field of psychognosy, namely in those cases where we are led by the thread of analogy in researching phenomena which are difficult to analyse. The more the analogy is grounded in related points, the more plausibly can we trust its guidance. Any knowledge of a related factor [*Moment*], even if it does not belong to the domain of psychology, will be of value in this context.

(h) Again, one cannot hope to achieve one's aim in the cases of psychognostic measurements in the sensory domain – and we shall see how such measurements are required for the construction of psychognosy – without using the knowledge of genetic psychology. I mention this only briefly, for it would be premature, at this stage, to conduct a thorough investigation of whether and how genetic psychology can help in overcoming the very awkward problems arising in this context.

Everything I explained so far referred specifically to the services which genetic psychology can render to psychognosy in the sensory domain.

The assistance in other domains might be less extensive, but certainly not negligible. For example, the arousal or the retaining of a sensory phenomenon not only serves in its observation, but also in observing other phenomena, which occur in regular correlation with this phenomenon.

And furthermore, it will be of extremely wide-ranging importance for psychognostic investigations to take into account those genetic laws concerning the conditions under which we are tempted to 8|9 deceive ourselves about our inner phenomena. ¦ For often we misinterpret inner perceptions grossly, in spite of their evidence [*Evidenz*], e.g. ZöLLNERian figures;[4a] perspective.

We take what is equal [*Gleiches*] for unequal, what is unequal for equal, plurality for unity (e.g. [when] two lines which phenomenally stick out not inconsiderably from one another are taken to be one, in spite of the space which separates them, and suchlike).

Even though much more ought still to be added, let these remarks be sufficient to substantiate our claim that in many cases psychognosy uses the knowledge of genetic psychology advantageously.

24. All the same, no matter how high one values these services, the services which psychognosy provides to genetic psychology are incomparably more valuable. As mentioned before, a genetic psychologist without psychognostic knowledge is like a physiologist without anatomical knowledge. Even so, one often finds researchers who dare to approach genetic psychological investigations in a pitiful ignorance of psychognosy, which, in turn, has the effect that all their efforts are in vain. There are people who conduct investigations into the causes of the phenomena of memory [*Gedächtniserscheinungen*] without knowing even the principal characteristic peculiarities of these phenomena.

Say, e.g., the peculiar modification through which something

10

which presented itself earlier as being present is seen (and judged) to be past. They treat this as if what is required is the explanation of a completely equal or merely somewhat weaker phenomenon. Others occupy themselves with the genesis of error and delusion [*Wahn*]. But they are in no way clear about what a judgment, what the evidence for a judgment and what a conclusion and its plausibility [*einleuchtende Folgerichtigkeit*] are. And, in misjudging the essential peculiarities of the normal states of affairs, they can delude themselves into thinking that these normal states, and the deviations from them, are sufficiently understood in their genetic laws, even though they have not touched the most basic differences between the normal and the deviant states of affairs at all.

The perfection of psychognosy will hence be one of the most essential steps in preparation for a genuinely scientific genetic 9|10 psychology. |

2

Elements of Consciousness

UNITY, NOT SIMPLICITY OF CONSCIOUSNESS

1. We divided psychology into psychognosy and genetic psychology, and briefly analysed both terms. On the basis of this analysis we were able to determine the natural order between the two disciplines.

2. It came to light that, in this natural order, psychognosy precedes genetic psychology. It cannot be doubted that, in a multitude of cases, progress in psychognosy is aided by genetic psychological knowledge. However, these services are insignificant in comparison to the dependency of genetic psychology on psychognosy, given by the former's constant need of being founded in psychognostic knowledge.

3. Our conceptual analysis was thus sufficient to arrive at this important conclusion.

However, for it to be satisfactory in all other respects, certain additional clarifications may be necessary.

4. We said that psychognosy aims to determine the *elements* of human consciousness and the ways in which they are connected. This implies that consciousness is something which consists of a multitude of parts.

5. This seems to contradict the old teaching that the soul is something strictly uniform and completely simple.

Admittedly, we are by no means the first ones to deny this. David HUME already contested this claim as being contrary to the clearest and most immediate experience.

If certain philosophers convince themselves that they are something simple, then he would not deny, says he, that this be the case for them. But of himself, and of everybody else (with the exception of this species of metaphysician), he says that he is convinced of their being nothing but a bundle of different ideas [*Vorstellungen*] which succeed one another with unspeakable speed, and which are 10:11 in constant flux and uninterrupted motion. In speaking of : 'elements' of consciousness, we seem to adopt his intention.

6. Yet I am far from finding HUME's account to be a completely accurate and correct expression of the true state of affairs.

(a) First of all, it is incorrect that our consciousness consists of nothing but ideas.
(b) And, in any case, the expression 'bundle'[5] is a very inaccurate term for what is truly the case. A 'bundle', strictly speaking, requires a rope or wire or something else binding it together. In the case of human consciousness it is out of the question that there is something of this sort, or even just something analogous to it. Yet if we take the expression more loosely, if we take it to denote only a multitude of things located side-by-side, clinging to, or merely touching one another, then we have to reject HUME's description as an essentially distorted picture of consciousness.
(c) No being side-by-side.
(d) No multitude of things, but most unambiguously a single thing, embracing the whole of an actual human consciousness.

This has already many times been demonstrated most rigorously. You will, e.g., find a detailed demonstration of this in Chapter IV ('On the Unity of Consciousness') of my *Psychology from an Empirical Standpoint*.

Here, I shall restrict my demonstration to a few remarks.

To claim that our present consciousness does not belong to one thing, but that it is distributed across a multitude of things, means that it does not fully consist in a real thing [*in einem Realen*] or in a collective of real things.

This, however, is completely inconceivable.

In looking at a picture, I have a presentation [*Vorstellung*] (phenomenon) of different colours. (It is impossible that one thing sees the one, another thing sees the other, a third thing

14

sees the third. For, which [would be] a noticing [*ein Bemerken*] of the order?)

11:12   I see and hear and recognize the difference. ¦

I imagine something and judge it.

I draw a conclusion.

I think something and want something.

I desire something for its own sake, and something else as a means. The whole of present consciousness is therefore decidedly embraced by a real unity [*eine Einheit der Realität*].

7. However unfortunate HUME's comparison of our consciousness to a bundle, he is undoubtably correct on one point:

Our consciousness does not present itself to our inner perception as something *simple*, but it shows itself as being composed of many parts.

Unity of reality is something different from simplicity of reality.

SEPARABLE AND DISTINCTIONAL PARTS

1. Yet, even though these parts never occur side by side like the parts of a spatial continuum, many amongst them can in some way be actually separated from one another like the parts of a spatial continuum. The sense in which one of these parts can be actually separated from another one is that the former, having existed earlier as belonging to the same real unit [*reale Einheit*] as the latter, continues to exist when the latter has ceased to be.

(a) [Examples of two-sided/mutual] actual separability:
    seeing and hearing,
    parts of seeing and parts of hearing, respectively,
    to see and to remember having seen.
(b) [Examples of] one-sided separability:
    seeing and noticing,
    seeing of a particular colour and presenting the concept [*Vorstellen des Begriffs*],
    concept and judgment,
    premises and conclusion, etc.

2. There is therefore no doubt: our consciousness is composite and

12:13   it allows us to distinguish parts, some of which ¦ can be actually separated from other ones, be it in a one- or a two-sided manner.

15

3. Again, within these parts one may be able to distinguish parts which are actually separable from one another, until one reaches parts where such a one- or two-sided separation can no longer take place. These parts could be called the elements of human consciousness.

4. However, even these ultimate actually separable parts, in some sense, can be said to have further parts.

5. Someone who believes in atoms believes in corpuscles which cannot be dissolved into smaller bodies. But even so he can speak of halfs, quarters, etc. of atoms: parts which are distinguishable even though they are not actually separable. To differentiate these from others, we may refer to them as distinctional [*distinktionelle*] parts. And, since distinguishing goes beyond actual separability, one could speak of parts or elements of elements.

6. We said that even though the, at some point in time, actual [*irgendwann wirklich*] consciousness of a human being does belong to a single real unit [*zu einer einzigen Realität*], this does not mean that it is something simple in virtue of this unity. Inner perception, however, does not display spatially diverging [*räumlich ausein-andertretende*] parts. Nevertheless, it [human consciousness] is undoubted composed of many parts, some of which, like seeing-hearing, are mutually separable, others [of which], like the seeing and the noticing of what is seen, are at least one-sidedly separable.

We found that often these parts themselves have parts which similarly can be actually separated from one another. Should this cease to be the case for certain parts, then one could speak of indivisible parts/elements of human consciousness.

7. But we said that it is possible to speak in some sense of further partitions [*Teilungen*] even in the case of these ultimate actually separable parts. These partitions would be found, not through actual separation, but through distinction.

I called them distinctional parts, in contrast to the actually
13|14 separable ones. And I explained the term by using the parts ⦙ which, according to atomists, are possessed by the smallest separable corpuscles.

8. Such merely distinctional parts were said also to be given in

16

human consciousness. Thus, here we have again, in a certain sense, parts of the elements. And as in the case of parts, so one may ultimately speak without contradiction of elements of elements (namely of the last merely distinctional parts of the last separable parts).

9. This too requires some elucidation, because the sort of distinctional parts exemplified (if there are atoms) by the upper and lower half, or by the four quarters of an atom, cannot be distinguished [in the context of] consciousness. After all, consciousness does not appear [in a] spatially extended [manner].

But the fact that there are no merely distinctional spatial parts does not exclude [the possibility of] there being any distinctional parts, in the same way in which the circumstance that there are no spatially separable parts did not exclude that there are other separable parts.

The simplest way, for the time being, to show you how this is conceivable is (I believe) to use a fictitious example.

A FICTITIOUS EXAMPLE

1. Man has the innate tendency to trust his senses. He believes in the actual existence of colours, tones and whatever else may be contained in a sensory presentation. After all, this is why one has spoken of outer perception, which, in its reliability, was placed side by side with the inner kind.

The experienced and, in particular, the scientifically enlightened [person] no longer has this trust. Let us return for a moment to the naïve initial state of our judging and imagine that what a so-called outer perception, say, e.g., a visual perception [*Gesichtswahrnehmung*], presents to us is real. What would be the parts which this reality would reveal itself to be composed of?

2. Well, it would primarily reveal itself as being composed of spatial parts, which consequently, at least in many cases, may be separable 14|15 from one another. ¦ But obviously [it would] also [show itself to be composed of] other parts of a completely different kind.

Let us assume that in the space embraced by intuition [*im durch die Anschauung umfassten Raume*] we were to find two blue spots, a grey spot and a yellow one. The two blue spots would be different from one another, and each one of them would be different from the yellow one. Yet there would be an essential difference between the

17

relation [*Verhältnis*] of the two blue ones to one another, and the relation of a blue one to the yellow one. We say that between the two blue ones there is a spatial difference, while between the blue and the yellow ones there is a spatial difference and a qualitative difference. Thus, in the latter case there are two differences, while in the former there is, apart from a relation of difference, also a relation of agreement. Concerning the blue spot, we will hence have to differentiate two things: the particular spatial determination [*Örtlichkeit*] and the particular quality, i.e. the particular colour. In the blue spot one must therefore distinguish a particularity of colour and a particularity of place [*Besonderheit des Orts*]. These particularities are thus actually contained in it, [they] are distinctional parts of them.

Let us go on! Comparing the grey spot, on the one hand, with the yellow one and, on the other, with a blue one, we will in both cases find the double difference which we noticed between the blue and the yellow spot, [namely] the spatial [difference] and the qualitative one. If we have one of the lighter shades of grey before us, it may happen that we find a difference between this grey and the blue which we are unable to discover between the grey and the yellow, and which we call a difference of lightness. As concerns lightness, we equate the given shade of grey with this yellow, whereas we say that it differs in lightness from the given blue.

So we would have a third thing [*ein drittes*] which could be distinguished in each of the three spots, and which would have to be referred to as a distinctional part of it:

(a) spatial particularity,
(b) particularity of lightness,
(c) particularity of quality.

3. Someone might say at this point: 'I admit that your speaking of parts is justified in this context. But why do you count them ¦ amongst the distinctional parts as opposed to the separable ones?

'The blue spot can be moved away without ceasing to be blue. It hence loses its given spatial particulatrity, while its qualitative particularity stays unchanged.

'Or, in changing colour, the blue spot can transform itself into a red one, while its spatial determination [*örtliche Bestimmtheit*] remains unchanged.

'Hence one should speak of actually separable, rather than distinctional, parts.'

15|16

4. This remark is erroneous. However, if the reflections up to now are new to you, you must be very careful to realize clearly the incorrectness of the claim.

If we have two spots before us which agree in lightness, in quality and maybe in other parts, and which differ only spatially, then they will appear as two, regardless of the manifold agreement. And, in fact, we do not only talk of two spatial determinations, but also of two individually different qualities [and] of two individually different lightnesses.

Indeed, if it were individually, i.e. in the full sense of the word, one and the same blue-thing* being here and there, how could the one continue to exist while the other, say, transforms itself into [a] red-thing. The spatial difference therefore individuates the otherwise identical spots.

What is the consequence if only the spatial particularity is changed? Can the same individual blue-thing still continue to exist? – Apparently not. Consequently, it is not the same individual blue-thing which previously possessed the spatial particularity, and which now continues to exist as separated from it. Rather, there is another individual thing [ein individuell anderes] similar only in kind but actually as truly different from it as two blue-things which simultaneously exist in different places are different from one another.

This individual blue-thing consequently proved itself to be actually inseparable from this individual place.

And, similar to the inseparability of this individual blue-thing from this individual place, it is impossible to separate this individual
16|17 lightness from ! this individual blue-thing, even though it may be possible to transform this blue-thing gradually into a brown-thing, or into any other colour-thing, with the lightness remaining the same. An equal lightness precisely does not mean that it is individually and actually the same.

In this way, it becomes clear that if we justifiably spoke of lightness, quality and spatial particularity in a coloured spot as three parts, then we could do so only in the sense of distinctional parts but not of actually separable ones.

---

* Brentano uses 'ein Blau', 'ein individuelles Blau', or 'ein Blaues' to refer to concrete individuals, which he also refers to as 'Flecken', i.e. 'spots'. Note, however, that Brentano treats the existence of such spots in external reality only as a useful fiction, for their real domain is in our sensory presentations (see also p.xviii).

5. We have thus found purely distinctional parts in the content – fictitiously taken to be real – of our visual experience [*Gesichtsempfindung*]. These parts do not appear in a spatial manner side by side, but are tied completely differently, in that they, one might say, penetrate one another. Lightness, quality and spatial particularity. I want to show you now how it would be possible to find further distinctional parts in this fictitious reality [*fingierten Wirklichkeit*], parts which would be connected by ties that would yet again have a wholly different character.

6. If I have a blue and a yellow point before me, I find that they differ spatially and in lightness as well as in quality.

Yet, at the same time, I do find some agreement with respect to quality.

This should become clear to every one of you if you think of a sound and compare it to the blue and the yellow point. Blue and yellow, in contrast to that sound, immediately appear as qualitatively related and in agreement, insofar as they are coloured. We thus notice here, on the one hand, a difference, and, on the other, an agreement with respect to the quality, i.e. with respect to that same component [*Stück*] which earlier we separated distinctionally as a unified part [*einheitlicher Teil*].

We say that the two qualities agree in their being colours, but that they differ *in that* the one is a blue and the other a yellow colour.

As far as the quality itself is concerned, we hence have agreement 17|18 as well as difference, i.e. partial agreement, partial difference. |

And what sort of parts are the ones mentioned here? Surely, if they were merely distinctional parts in the previous case, then the same must be true be in the present case. After all, there cannot be a colour in general, [i.e. one] which is neither yellow nor blue nor in any other way more precisely qualitatively determined.

And just as little is it possible that a colour individually remains the same *qua* colour, while it has ceased to be yellow and instead is now blue.

7. We are therefore dealing here, as before, with a purely distinctional separation of parts.

At the same time, it is unquestionably the case that we are here dealing with a connection [*Verbindung*] of parts which has an essentially different character.

When we distinguish quality and spatial particularity, we are

20

dealing with two specific determinations which are of a different genus, and which, penetrating one another in a manner peculiar to them, mutually contribute to their individualization. In the present case, however, we are dealing with two determinations, one super-ordinate to the other, which determine (one simply less than the other) the thing from the same side, so to speak. In other words, we are dealing with what, in the strict sense, is called a generic logical determination [*logische Gattungsbestimmtheit*] and a specific logical difference [*logische spezifische Differenz*].

It is peculiar to this that distinctionally we also only have a one-sided separability. For if redness [*Röte*] is the same as red colour, i.e. if colour is the generic determination and red the specific difference, then it is clear that, even though the generic determination colour is distinctionally separable from red, the specific difference red cannot likewise be separated from colour, [i.e. it is clear] that the difference is rather equal to the whole of the determination of [the] species [*Speziesbestimmtheit*] (genus and difference taken together).

8. Hence, in using our fictitious example of the reality corresponding to our visual perception, we have shown there to be *several*, essentially different classes of purely distinctional parts.

9. Before we commence to examine human consciousness with respect to the question about distinctional parts, let us again create a fiction similar to the one in which we assumed that our experiential presentation [*Empfindungsvorstellung*] constitutes a correct picture [*getreues Abbild*] of a reality. ¦ Let us assume fictitiously that the same holds of a presentation which many count as itself belonging to sensory presentation, but which in fact really deserves to be called a presentation of original association. Explanation using a spoken word, indeed a spoken syllable, a melodic succession, a visual experience [*Anschauung*] of movement.

What is special here is that certain qualities, determined more closely in one way or another, do not occur in the manner in which qualities occur in experience, but that they occur modified in the way of being presented as being past [*als vergangen vorgestellt*], and more and more past.

If we were to think that this presentation corresponds to a reality, then it would not be a sound, but a past sound [*gewesener Ton*], not a colour, but a past colour, not a spatial particularity, but a past spatial particularity and so forth. 'Past' is not a determiningly enriching

21

[*determinierende bereichernde*], but a modifying determination of 'sound'. Sound is not strictly but only modifyingly contained in the past sound, which is why it cannot be gained from the latter by a proper, simple distinguishing [*einfaches Distinguieren*] (noticing), but only by a modifying one. If we wish to say that 'sound' is a distinctional part of 'past sound', we can only do so in a considerably deviant and looser sense.[6]

10. And so we have been able to identify distinctional parts of greatly differing character in those real objects which we fictitiously assumed to exist as corresponding to our sensory presentations. Above all, we can divide distinctional parts into two classes: (i) distinctional parts in the strict sense and (ii) parts which can be obtained through modifying distinction. Then again, we can distinguish two classes of strictly distinctional parts, of which one – because a commonly accepted scientific term is missing – may be called the class of mutually pervading [*sich durchwohnende*] parts, and the other, the class of logical parts.

11. These remarks should demonstrate that, even if purely distinctional spatial parts cannot occur in the context of human consciousness (as they do with a possibly existing atom), distinctional parts of another, and possibly ¦ in many ways differing character, are nevertheless still conceivable.

19¦20

As a matter of fact, distinctional parts belonging to the different classes which we have just put together are also to be found in human consciousness; indeed, they reveal themselves in even more manifold ways.

DISTINCTIONAL PARTS IN THE STRICT SENSE

Mutually Pervading Parts

1. The following are the mutually pervading parts in the act of judging 'There is a truth':

(a) affirmative quality
(b) the being directed [*Gerichtetsein*] upon the object 'truth',
(c) self-evidence,
(d) the apodeictic modality,[7]
    that there is a truth is recognized as being necessarily true.

For if it were false that there is a truth, it would be true that there is no truth, hence there would be a truth and yet also no truth, which is contradictory. This is not the same as 'evidence' [*Evidenz*], for 'I am' is evident to me, but this is not clear to me as being a necessary truth.

2. Thus we have in one [single] act four mutually pervading particularities, and maybe we might be able to discover in the same act an even greater number of mutually pervading distinctional parts. But for the present purpose, these are quite sufficient.

Logical Parts

1. For example, in an affirmation, that it is an accepting judging[8] and in the judging, that it is a relation (of consciousness) [(*Bewusstseins-*) *beziehung*] which is judging and intentional. What we emphasized earlier as being a general peculiarity [*Eigenheit*] of all logical parts, namely their being only one-sidedly distinctionally separable, is again true. Let us consider another example: experiencing, ¦ seeing, seeing-red [*Rotsehen*]; i.e. experiencing visual (colour-sensing) experiencing, and seeing-red [type of] seeing [rotsehendes Sehen] (red-sensing experiencing of colour).

20¦21

2. These two classes of distinctional parts in the strict sense are old acquaintances. But, in the domain of consciousness, there are two further ones.

One is the psychical relation which is essential for any consciousness, the other the inseparable connection of the primary and the concomitant psychical relation.

Parts of the Intentional Pair of Correlates[8a]

1. Hence, the peculiarity which, above all, is generally characteristic of consciousness, is that it shows always and everywhere, i.e. in each of its separable parts, a certain kind of relation, relating a subject to an object. This relation is also referred to as 'intentional relation'. To every consciousness belongs essentially a relation.

2. As in every relation, two correlates can be found here. The one correlate is the act of consciousness, the other is that [thing] which it is directed upon.

23

Seeing and what is seen,
Presenting and what is presented,
Wanting and what is wanted,
Loving and what is loved,
Denying and what is denied etc.

As highlighted already by ARISTOTLE,[9] these correlates display the peculiarity that the one alone is real, [whereas] the other is not something real [nichts Reales]. A person who is being thought [ein gedachter Mensch] is as little something real as a person who has ceased to be [gewesener Mensch]. The person who is being thought hence has no proper cause and cannot properly have an effect. But, when the act of consciousness (the thinking of the person) is effected, the person who is being thought (the non-real correlate of the person) coexists [ist mit da]. The two correlates are only distinctionally separable from one another.

21:22 And so we have here again two purely distinctional ¦ parts of the pair of correlates, one of which is real, the other [of which] is not.

3. Explanation of the term object: some internal object-like thing [ein innerlich Gegenständliches] is meant. It need not correspond to anything outside.

To avoid misunderstandings, one may call it 'in-dwelling' [inwohnendes] or 'immanent' object.

This is something (a) generally and (b) exclusively characteristic of consciousness.

If, as we commonly believe, there is an unconscious world of bodies with sensible qualities (or, instead, with a mass of [qualities] of whatever nature non-intuitive to us, which fill certain spaces), then it will certainly partake in many other kinds of relations, like that of part and whole, agreement and difference, cause and effect, and so forth.

But it absolutely does not take part in this intentional relation. Hence 'psychical relation'. Clearly, this brings some intricacy to the domain of consciousness not given in the sensory phenomena which we have been considering.

The Primary and the Secondary Psychical Relation

1. And the intricacy is increased even further by the second factor which we identified as a general fact about consciousness, namely

24

the inseparable connection of a primary and a concomitant psychical relation.

Every consciousness, upon whatever object it is primarily directed, is concomitantly directed upon itself [*geht nebenher auf sich selbst*]. In the presenting [*im Vorstellen*] of the colour hence simultaneously a presenting of this presenting. ARISTOTLE already [emphasizes] that the psychical phenomenon contains the consciousness of itself.[10]

2. Many have denied this in recent times. [It is claimed that] one often sees something and is not conscious of seeing it; that one is thinking something, but is not conscious of thinking it.

22¦23 ¦ Accordingly, [it is claimed,] one can be drawing a conclusion and neither be able to give the premises, nor to give an account of the event in any other way.

3. Indeed, some [go] even further. They (like, e.g. Albert LANGE) approvingly quote one of GOETHE's sayings: 'He never thought of thinking'. Thus one must no doubt assume they believe that such a secondary relation of consciousness is never, and in no case, united with the primary one.

4. However, as far as GOETHE's remark is concerned, it would be such an obvious absurdity when taken literally that not even the highest reverence could bring us to agree to it.

He never thought of thinking? he tells us. But isn't he himself in that very moment thinking of it, or does he speak of it without thinking of it? And did he speak without thinking what he was saying, whenever he mentioned thinking, knowing and erring in *Faust* or wherever else? No, surely we are not allowed to interpret GOETHE in such a foolish way. He might have wished to say that he never reflected about thinking, or that he never observed the thinking currently taking place in him, both of which would not be contrary to what we have put forward.

A mathematician who is absorbed in his calculation focuses the whole of his attention on the numerical relations. He certainly does not observe his thinking, rather he only perceives it on the side [*nebenher*].

5. If one takes into account that coexisting in consciousness [*mit ins Bewusstsein fallen*] is different from being specifically noticed, and from being comprehended with the clarity which allows a correct

25

determination and description, then the illusion that some psychical activity can be devoid of the secondary psychical relation disappears completely and with utmost ease.

Whoever sees a lark in the blue of the sky does therefore not yet notice it, and hence will just as little notice his seeing of the lark, even though his seeing of the lark is concomitantly experienced [*mitempfinden*] by him. However, were he, at some point, not only to see the lark, but also to notice it, then he would certainly notice ! simultaneously that he sees it. If someone sees a human face, he sees all the features and colours which it contains, but this will not in any way enable him to identify them all by means of a correct description. And if he makes a portrait of this face, he may believe it to be a very good likeness, while he really has created something which in colour and shape is so different from the original that nobody can recognize the person. To see is different from being clear about what is seen. And thus, the concomitant experience [*mitempfinden*] of the seeing will be different from being clear about this concomitantly experienced seeing.

23:24

If someone thinks a concept, it is undeniable that he has concomitantly thought all the features contained in it; but he might have noticed so few of them clearly that he is unable to define it, indeed, that he considers a false definition as being correct, until the error is pointed out to him.

In this way, it can understandably happen that someone draws conclusions without being able to account at all for the thought process in a precise and faultless manner. It so happened that PLATO wanted to make [the drawing of] conclusions generally subordinate to the processes of recalling from memory [*Wiedererinnerung*], even though the two have so little in common. Yet he did draw conclusions in the exactly same manner as we do. And, like us, he did not draw them in the sort of unconscious manner in which the primary relation of thinking would not have been tied to a secondary relation, directed at the thinking itself.

6. The fact which was asserted already by ARISTOTLE is hence justified. Regardless of the few people who have been led astray, no doubt can be raised about it. The fact that there is no consciousness without any intentional relation at all is as certain as the fact that, apart from the object upon which it is primarily directed, consciousness has, on the side, itself as an object.[11] This is, in an essential way, part of the nature of every psychical act.

7. This actual dual-relation gives rise to the increased intricacy which I spoke of, an intricacy which creates the impression that consciousness is even richer in distinctional parts than the sensory phenomena which we have studied earlier.

24|25
(a) One easily notices that we are here dealing with something other than the connection of logical parts. None of the parts here is a generic determination to which a difference would be added.
(b) The nature of these parts also differs in an essential way from that of mutually pervading parts. We have distinguished several mutually pervading parts in the act of judging 'There is a truth', like, e.g., affirmation and evidence, but all of them belonged to the relation to one and the same object, to truth as truth.

The present case is completely different. The experiencing of the colour and the concomitant experiencing of this experiencing are directed towards [gehen auf] different objects.

The present case is, in this respect, similar to those separable parts which we discerned earlier in the psychical domain, like, e.g., seeing and hearing and simultaneous seeing of different parts of one and the same picture.

Whereas the separation of the parts considered there can only be actual, the parts considered here can only be separated distinctionally. This is why, having referred to the former as actually separable psychical parts, it was probably not wholly inappropriate to call the latter inseparable (distinctional) ones.

8. The four genera [Gattungen] of distinctional parts in the strict sense which we said were to be found in the domain of consciousness hence are:

(1) [the] mutually pervading ones,
(2) [the] logical ones,
(3) the parts of the intentional pair of correlates,
(4) merely distinctional parts of the psychical *Diploseenergie*, [primary and secondary psychical relation], leaving open the question whether this dual-relation might not again be divisible into two [further] classes.

27

DISTINCTIONAL PARTS IN THE MODIFIED SENSE

1. All that remains to be done now is to talk about the parts in the domain of consciousness which are to be gained by modifying distinction.

25:26   2. In providing examples for the logical parts which can be found in the domain ¦ of consciousness, we listed, amongst other things:

Experiencing, seeing, seeing-red [*Rotsehen*]. And in doing so, we noticed that these examples displayed the peculiarity of all logical parts, namely the only one-sided separability of the generic determination.

We noticed that the difference always presupposes, [or] includes the generic specification, and that thus, in content, it is equal to the species.

3. Regardless of the correctness of this remark, some people might be tempted to claim that it is incorrect.

Experiencing, they might say, differentiates itself as an experiencing of colour, sound, etc. The seeing, i.e. the experiencing of [what is] coloured [differentiates itself] as a seeing of blue, red, yellow and so forth. These acts differentiate themselves according to the objects and the differences of the objects like colour, blue, red. But the objects do not contain the generic determination experiencing, seeing.

Hence we have here a case where logical parts are mutually separable.

4. The refutation [of this] lies in the fact that it is not colour but colour experience [*Farbempfindung*] which is the difference that marks off seeing from other kinds of experiencing. If colour were the difference of seeing, then seeing would have to be a coloured experiencing, and thus would itself have to be coloured, which is not the case.

And similarly it is not correct that red is the difference which marks off seeing-red from other kinds of seeing, for otherwise seeing-red would itself have to be something red.

5. But even though the objection was based on an error, it did touch upon something true.

28

ARISTOTLE already said that the seeing subject [*das Sehende*] is, in a manner of speaking, coloured.[12]

If the seeing subject really were 'coloured', if it really had the colour in and on itself, then we could indeed distinctionally separate the difference from the generic determination in the case of seeing *qua* coloured experiencing, and *vice versa*. But it is only 'in a manner of speaking' coloured, the colour is not really in it and therefore cannot be referred to as a distinctional part of seeing, in the strict sense.

26:27
But, by colour being at least 'in a manner of speaking' in the seeing subject, it turns out that we have here something similar to what we noticed in the phenomenon ¦ of the past sound, which equally, in a manner of speaking, contained the sound. And, as in the case of the sound, it will thus be possible to obtain the colour as a part of seeing by modifying distinction.

This is why colour is obviously in some way simpler than the seeing of the colour, in the same way as the phenomenon sound is simpler than that of the past sound.

6. And what is true of the real member of the intentional relation also holds for its non-real correlate. 'Seen colour' [*gesehene Farbe*] contains, in a manner of speaking, colour, not as a distinctional part in the strict sense, but as a part to be obtained from it by modifying distinction.

7. Here we have the proof that such distinctional parts also exist in the domain of consciousness. The objects in the act and in its intentional correlate can be referred to as such parts.

8. And furthermore, the parts of these parts will add themselves as improper distinctional parts; e.g. like sound as part of a sound which is sensorily presented as being past.

9. It is necessary for psychognosy to go back also to the purely distinctional elements,

(a) otherwise there is no clear description,
(b) otherwise an unspeakable, endless proliferation is created. There would be innumerable names (at least as many as there are points in the visual field),

29

(c) furthermore, and in particular, the following: it is the distinguishing of a purely distinctional part in which lies the essence of [certain] special separable parts.

These [special separable parts] are as manifold as the distinctional parts which are distinguished, and they are to be defined through them. Thus it is clear that the complete survey of the actually separable parts is indivisible from the survey of the purely distinctional ones. |

27|28

30

3

THE CORRECT METHOD OF THE PSYCHOGNOST

INTRODUCTION

1. Even though the task of psychognosy is much easier than that of genetic psychology, it is nevertheless in itself a difficult one. This is sufficiently revealed by the state in which psychognosy still finds itself today.

For one thing, it shows considerable lacunae. Many questions are usually left completely untouched. Even if they are touched on, they are not approached in a genuinely scientific manner. And as far as those other questions, which are treated with some thoroughness, are concerned, one finds that almost everyone is fighting everybody else, even themselves.

2. Where so many fail in their undertakings, how could we approach the matter without some apprehension?

In any case, like someone who sets out for a dangerous sea voyage, it will be beneficial to find out, if possible, the location of the cliffs and sandbanks on which one might get stranded.

3. To achieve his aim, the psychognost must achieve a multitude of things.

(a) He has to experience [*erleben*],
(b) he has to notice [*bemerken*],
(c) he has to fix [*fixieren*] what he notices, in order to collect it,
(d) he has to generalize inductively;
(e) where the necessity or impossibility of a unification of certain elements becomes clear from the concepts themselves, he must intuitively grasp these general laws;

(f) finally, we can add that he has to make deductive use of what he gained, in one way or another, from general laws. By doing this, he will be able to solve many questions concerning the elements which otherwise he would scarcely have been able to answer.

4. Let us now expand somewhat on each of the designated points [i.e. on each of the desiderata for the correct method of a psychognost] and investigate, in each case, how far we can avoid psychognostical imperfections. |

28¦29

EXPERIENCING

1. Above all, the psychognost must experience, i.e. his inner perception must register [*erfassen*], if not simultaneously, then at least successively, a wealth of facts of human consciousness if he is not to lack the material necessary for his investigations.

2. In experiencing there is initially no room for error. Yet [there may be] an incompleteness due to the narrower constraints of one's own life as opposed to the domain of human experiences in general.

3. However, it is not the case that each one of these constraints must be to the completeness of psychognosy. For otherwise, how could or would the individual [person] experience in himself all that is humanly possible [to experience]?

(a) One does not need to experience the more complicated states in order to experience all the elements;
(b) again, one certainly does not need to experience all the separable elements, in order to survey them, provided only that all the purely distinctional elements of these separable elements are brought into one's consciousness.

I need not have made every simple judgment, [or] to have cherished every wish, in order to understand the person who expresses them to me.

If I did experience them, then they would not even be particularly registered by me *qua* psychognost, but [they would be] comprehended concomitantly [*mit umfasst*]. – For otherwise, I would find myself carrying out the useless, long-winded and indeed neverending task of trying to characterize the classes to which each of them belong.

(c) Indeed, we can go even further! Not even all the purely distinctional elements need to be present in the inner life [*inneres Leben*] of a psychognost for him to carry out his task almost as well as if they were present. For example, in the case of spatial elements.

Explanation: neither spatial nor temporal intuition are infinite.

But our conceptual determinations [*begriffliche Bestimmungen*] expand [them] to the infinite. ¦

29¦30

(d) It would not be very detrimental [to psychognosy] if the intuitive part [*anschaulicher Teil*] of one person were more limited than that of another. Yet there are other cases where the lack of certain experiences does indeed bring about an incompleteness in psychognostic knowledge.

So, [for example,] the lack of smell,

the lack of hearing, [or] of sight,

[and] indeed partial deficiencies [*teilweiser Mangel*], as in the colour-blind person, or in those people who do not see colour differences in the narrow sense, but who see the world as in a copper etching.

4. The danger that the psychognost cannot achieve his task due to lack of sufficient experiential material is hence essentially confined to these cases of a rudimentary inner life.

5. They are not infrequent. It is said that, on average, one out of twelve individuals does not see all the colours. But this is inexact, for it varies between different peoples.

For many, this figure is too high, while for others (Nordic ones) it is even too low.

6. In any case, there is no general danger. And each individual can easily dispel any doubt as to whether he might belong to this group, and then proceed courageously to the study of psychognosy.

7. And – I must add – should someone realize that he actually suffers from such an elementary limitation, then he should not lose heart and retreat from studying psychognosy. He will still have the largest part in common with all of humanity. And if the gap in his psychognostic knowledge, which will necessarily result from this source, is the only one he has, then he will have all justification to consider himself as

33

the most knowledgable psychognost who has lived, and – may I say – who will ever live.

8. Cases like that of Laura BRIDGMAN [13] [are] fortunately rare. Even rarer [are cases where] there is [no] further psychical development despite the obstacle. [In such a case,] mind you, psychognosy is out of the question. But if, as in the case of Laura, a psychical
30¦31 development occurs after all, then there ¦ would still remain the widest and most rewarding field for psychognostic studies.

9. So, the first point has the least serious consequences:

(a) no error is involved,
(b) where there is an incompleteness, it is only in a narrowly limited area, and without any all too serious disadvantages for the rest.

10. Much more serious disadvantages for psychognosy will, in general, arise from the second of the components demanded [for the correct method of a psychognost].

NOTICING

1. We have said: secondly, the psychognost has to notice. As we mentioned earlier, and as everyone can easily convince himself over and over again, one can experience something quite well without noticing it. [This can happen] by something being contained in the manifold of what simultaneously falls into our inner perception and what is concomitantly genuinely perceived, but which we do not notice in any way at all. And in that sense it is as good as non-existent for the purposes of psychognosy.

2. If the psychognost's work is not to be flawed with an essential incompleteness, he must not only experience a wide range of phenomena of human consciousness, but he has to notice sufficiently the particular experiences and their essential parts.

3. Mind you, many important things may not be noticed by him, but this does not necessarily imply that he is in error.
  There is as little error involved in not noticing psychical processes as there was in not experiencing them. There is no erroneous noticing, like there is never any inner perception at all [which is]

34

bare of evidence [*Evidenz*]. Yet, not noticing may easily lead to incompleteness in much more crucial respects than [what could arise from] never experiencing colour or sound. |

31|32

4. Many people may possibly be surprised about what I am saying here. The loss of certain important classes of experiences due to a rudimentary functioning of the senses is understandable and leads to a rudimentary psychognosy. But should the lack of noticing bring about similar, or even bigger shortcomings? Should there be classes of important elements of consciousness which remain unknowable for the whole of one's life due to the lack of noticing?

Certainly [this would be so], if a certain kind of element were to occur only once in our consciousness! But that is not the way things are. The elements recur constantly, or, at least from time to time, in our perceptions. And if at one time they occur in a manner in which they cannot easily be noticed, then they will occur another time under conditions which are so favourable that we are immediately struck by them. For example, the black spot in our field of vision which occurs when a lark floats in the blue [expanse] of the sky may be difficult to notice: but at another time we will have a (the same) black-thing [*ein (dasselbe) Schwarz*] clearly before us, like on a window-pane, and this time the element is noticed.

5. But whoever thinks like that is wrong. It is not only likely, but, I think, it can be rigidly proven that our consciousness contains elements which are and will never be noticed by any psychognost. And we may add that these are elements the knowledge of which would be of incomparably bigger psychological interest than the knowledge of all the colour and sound phenomena taken together. This is certainly the case for the element which individuates our consciousness. But this just as an aside. Later, when dealing more thoroughly with the matter, we shall clarify what, at present, must necessarily appear to you as being rather opaque.

6. The completeness of psychognosy is not only impaired by the cases in which something falling into the sphere of our experience is virtually unnoticeable. Instead, it must be said that, even though recurring again and again in our consciousness, much of what does not belong to the virtually unnoticeable has, as a matter of fact, never

32|33 been noticed by most people, | including psychognosts who eagerly endeavoured to analyse the phenomena.

35

In the course of our investigations, we will have ample occasion to confirm this. The fact that under certain circumstances one may not notice the individual thing one experiences hence harbours the indisputable danger of severe incompleteness for psychognosy.

7. In the face of this danger, the question arises how best to protect oneself from it? And [furthermore] how one could avoid, in particular, living continually in the uncertainty of whether one has overlooked the most essential pieces, and thus given only the most rudimentary list of the psychical elements[?]

8. This question is closely connected with one concerning the conditions under which noticing occurs, and those under which it does not. But this is a psychogenetic question, and thus we cannot give an exact and exhaustive answer. At any rate, it will be quite taxing just to determine in an inexact manner some relevant conditions which are at least on average correct. Yet, no matter how unsatisfactory for our theoretical interests these [inexact psychogenetic] conditions may be, and no matter how little they allow us to draw infallible conclusions in any particular case, one can justifiably claim that for the practical purposes of conducting extended and frequently repeated experiments, they essentially compensate for the lack of more exact knowledge.

9. Above all, we must ensure that we keep in mind exactly what the aim of our investigations is. We are asking about the conditions of noticing. By noticing we mean an inner perception, in fact an explicit perception of what was implicitly contained in the perception of [as performed by] our consciousness [*Wahrnehmung unseres Bewusstseins*].

10. Something which is not implicitly perceived by us does not occur in our consciousness.

But that does not at all mean that it is explicitly perceived. A
33|34   clarification of this distinction seems to be desirable. ┆

Perception is an acceptance [*Anerkennung*]. And if the accepted thing is a whole with parts, then the parts are all, in a certain manner, concomitantly accepted. The denial of any of them would contradict the acceptance of the whole. Yet the individual part is, for this reason, by no means accepted [–] let alone judged [–] specifically (by itself) and in particular.

36

A comparison with the case of denial may highlight this point even further. In a simple denial of something, the part is not likewise an object of a denial.

Indeed, there is not even an implicit concomitant denial of the part.

There is however an implicit concomitant denial of everything belonging to the extension of the concept.

But it is obvious that not all of this is implicitly judged. And this highlights the importance of the difference between the state of judging merely implicitly and that of doing so explicitly.

11. Noticing and perceiving are occcasionally said to be a kind of predicating, in fact sometimes a negative and sometimes an affirmative one.

For example, the perceiving of a difference, the noticing of a distinction. To perceive or notice that one thing is identical with another thing. When I speak of noticing in this context, I have in mind only simple accepting judgments. Yet, I am not denying that in many cases such negative and affirmative predications are also intimately tied to the acts of noticing with which we are concerned here, and that they are no less infallible than these acts.

12. Let me add a word of clarification about the connection of the concept of noticing used here with some other relevant concepts.

What I have in mind are the concepts of:

to be struck [by something] [*auffallen*],
to take note [of something] [*sich merken*],
34|35   to pay attention [*aufmerken*].[14]

13. '[Somebody] noticing [something]' is, according to how we specified 'noticing', not the same as [somebody] being struck [by something].

To be struck by something is an emotional state [*Gemütszustand*]; 'to be displeased', 'to be astonished' are expressions with similar meaning, possibly just more intense ones.

It is correct that noticing and being struck are often connected with one another.

A change often leads to noticing the difference between the state of affairs before and that after [the change].

And a change is very often also striking. Whatever is new, extraordinary or breaking the habit is, after all, what strikes one.

37

But this does not mean that they [i.e. noticing and being struck] are one and the same. It would be equally erroneous to believe that something must first strike us in order to be noticed. On the contrary, nothing will strike us which has not already been noticed by us. However, being struck by something which has been noticed can lead us to investigate it more closely. To be struck by something can hence lead to many new explicit perceptions.

14. It would also be wrong to confuse 'noticing' with 'taking note'. The latter is to make an impression on one's mind, it is to make sure that what is currently recognized will be at one's disposal at a later time.

We will have to deal with this later. 'To take note of something' is not necessarily tied to 'noticing' itself. Something could be noticed without one particularly taking note of it. And, even though being properly noticed, it could very well completely escape our knowledge at a later stage.

There is a further difference. It is possible to say 'to take note carefully [of something]'. There are gradations in this case.

Not so in the case of noticing. Here we always have evidence, and evidence does not have degrees.

15. Noticing is also different from paying attention, even though it stands in close relation to it.

We are speaking of paying attention where we desire to notice something which is currently happening in us, or which is about to happen, and which, presumably, we also want to take note of, and where we are driven by this desire to create favourable dispositions for this to occur. One can thus say that we are speaking of paying
35:36 attention where it is our aim to notice.

(However, this is to use 'noticing' in a wider sense.)

Many [people] simply wanted to say that paying attention is [nothing but] the desire (or the will) to notice. But this is insufficient. One could have the desire to notice a hundred new impressions which are to be expected at that moment, but that would not mean that one would be paying attention to them. Indeed, this would be impossible, because the dispositions which one would adopt to notice some of these impressions would make it more difficult to notice the others, and everything would, so to speak, lead to a state of complete scattering. There is [incidentally] also [such] a thing [as] being

38

attentive against one's will, *nota bene* against the *actus imperatus*, not *elicitus*. Apart from the fact that not every desire is 'will'.

16. Yet, it is of utmost importance to consider what we are doing when we pay attention, and in which cases this is, or isn't successful.

It is not as if attentiveness could be an indispensable precondition for noticing. How should one come to notice? The desire to notice belongs to attentiveness, but attentiveness is not the immediate preparatory disposition, or, in any case, not the whole of it. And thus, if, independently of desire, the essential most immediate conditions are met, noticing will take place without a prior paying of attention.

But as we want to determine successful conditions [for noticing] by paying attention, we will all the same be able to make important observations [by means of paying attention].

17. Those cases where our aim is for someone else to notice something internally [– i.e.] where we, so to speak, pay attention for them in arousing and guiding their attentiveness [–] are similarly to be considered.

18. Indeed, these cases are probably the most instructive. We know exactly what we are driving at when we are guiding someone else, and we will therefore achieve our aim much more easily (pre-supposing they have the same [psychical] make-up as we do).

It will be similar to those cases where we disclose a discovery to someone else. This can be achieved with much more ease than the search for new discoveries.

36:37   19. So let us see what we are doing when we intend ¦ to lead others to notice something (and let us investigate when this is successful and when it isn't).

20. Naturally, not absolutely all the cases of us trying to make someone else notice something will be taken into account.

(a) In particular, we will not take into account the cases where we are not dealing with a noticing in our narrowly specified sense. [Thus, we will not discuss,] for example, the noticing of a difference, i.e. the noticing that something is not the same as something else (a negative predication), or the noticing that something is something else (positive predication) – except in

39

those cases where such knowledge is somehow interwoven with those simple perceptions we are interested in.

b) Furthermore, we will not discuss our preparatory contribution to noticing involved in our arousing [*erwecken*] the phenomenon which either is to be noticed, or which has something on it to be noticed.

Let us assume the phenomenon is present. What can we do to notice it?

21. Here we can distinguish between less immediate and more immediate factors. First of all [let us speak] of the former. (Maybe [it might be] better the other way around!)

(a) Above all, we will not attempt to carry out indiscriminately each of these experiments on every kind of subject.

In the same way as we would never try to bring an animal to notice the peculiarity of the so-called evident judgments, even though they seem to have such judgments, we will not try to do so in the case of:

a very small infant,

a mentally handicapped person suffering from flight of ideas [*Ideenflucht*[14a]]

or a lunatic.

To have any hope of success, we will approach normal, sufficiently mature, i.e. by nature suitable individuals.

(b) Moreover, if we are dealing with what is more or less difficult to notice, we will take care to perfect the natural dispositions through practice. This will, in particular, be achieved through practice in noticing. The skills ¦ of noticing can be perfected through practice on a general level as well as in the context of specific domains one is interested in. Someone who was engaged a lot in psychognostic studies will be led more easily than a novice to notice something which is difficult to notice. Someone who has worked continuously in psychognosy will, *ceteris paribus*, have an advantage over someone who did concern himself with psychognostic studies, but ceased to do so a long time ago.

It has been established by many experiments that practising facilitates the ease of noticing not just on a general level, but also

37|38

in particular domains. In the domain of the senses, in particular, one has found some noteworthy facts. There is a specific training through practice of the [capacity for] noticing not just for each of the senses [themselves], but also for each of their branches [*Teilgebiete*]. For example, in the region of clearest vision[,] in the lateral regions of the eye (ladies); in the case of the 'skin sense', experiments with needles of compasses have been carried out, [and it has been found that] the differences soon became much more pronounced if practising had been carried out on the same region of the skin. NOLTEMANN found that, within a very short period of time, his sensibility for differences in certain regions was doubled, indeed quadrupled. Yet his skilfulness in other regions [of the skin] remained almost unchanged by this.

But not in all [skin regions].

Curious behaviour of homologous limbs.

Practising the left upper arm induced a concomitant practising of the corresponding skin region of the right upper arm etc.

In contrast, no instances of such concomitant practising for skin regions of the same arm, with the exception, perhaps, of immediately neighbouring regions.

Practising the little finger of the left hand was without any noticeable influence on the skin of the forearm.

Given this, one will naturally [try] to give rise in appropriate ways to [the relevant] practice if dealing with something which is difficult to notice.

In doing so, one need not proceed indefinitely. On the contrary, at least in the domain of the senses, one has noticed that the advantage ¦ gained through practice is virtually maximal after a relatively short period of time. However, it does need refreshing from time to time. What is almost more important than to practice noticing is to take care that there is no practice in not-noticing. In the same way as there is a habit not to form associations when saying the Lord's Prayer, a habit can be formed in certain cases not to pay attention to a phenomenon, but instead focus one's attention on something else. Such habits become a sort of second nature. They appear to be as powerful as an immutable inherited law, and where one does succeed in overcoming them, the process will be difficult and slow. For example, the habit of most people to pay attention only to what lies in their region of clearest vision and at the distance to which they are accommodated. This

38¦39

41

is why many [have] the greatest difficulties in noticing double images. How can one achieve it?

Another way of preparing [oneself] is to use a practising habit [*vorübende Gewohnheit*]. Habit is most powerful in the same or similar situations. In order to bring someone to notice something which is difficult to notice, he is to be placed under conditions under which he habitually tends to notice [things, conditions like]: [. . .]

pacing up and down in the study,

opening the eyes widely,

lifting up the head,

pricking up the ears,

the muscle sensations in a familiar space at a familiar time, etc.

(c) It is obvious that, for noticing, the state of being awake is preferable to that of being asleep, in particular, if the noticing is to be brought about intentionally [*durch Absicht*].

No doubt, one notices a lot of things in dreams, and what is thus noticed is of interest even for the psychologist.

However, no one has made any new psychognostic discoveries while they were asleep.

And, indeed, nobody has made such discoveries if not by intentionally guiding themselves towards noticing according to a carefully thought out plan. ¦

Weakness of will-power over the limbs and the inner operations is characteristic of sleep.

This is much less the case, both inwardly and outwardly, when one is half asleep (somnambulism). In this case, one can often influence dreams and guide the attention of the person who dreams. But in comparison to the waking state [this is] still poor.

(d) Likewise, freshness is to be preferred to the state of exhaustion or to that of fatigue.

One cannot properly pay attention if one is very fatigued. If one has been paying attention for too long, one is, despite increased practice, less able than ever to notice something, in particular if one deals with something which is difficult to notice.

(e) Another condition which evidently has to be taken into account is the presence of an appropriate emotional state.

Affect, fear, anger and other passionate emotions confuse everything one inwardly undertakes in order to notice something which is difficult to notice. Since these phenomena themselves

39|40

42

must be studied, this is something which creates particular difficulties for psychology. We will return to this later.

(f) Moreover, it will be part of the less immediate preparations to exclude anything distracting in order to focus, as one says, the attention on one point. This has to do with the narrow nature [*Enge*] of consciousness. We will see that particular difficulties will arise from this for those particular cases in which such an exclusion is impossible.

(g) There is yet another important obstacle to be removed.

Existing prejudices have to be destroyed. Otherwise it will not be possible to let someone notice something, even though the conditions have been made as favourable as possible in all other respects. Noticing is suspended, like it is with many who let themselves be confused by paralogisms in not recognizing the principle of the excluded middle. ¦

40¦41

Explanation: Zeno-type arguments and so forth, HEGEL, TRENDELENBURG.[14b, 15]

22. I have seen the most remarkable examples. GOMPERZ: Evidence.[16]

23. Important in this context is the 'prejudice rooted in habit'. Examples [of facts which are not noticed because of this sort of prejudice]:

(1) That judgment is a second relation, fundamentally different from that of presenting [*Vorstellen*].

The [counteractive] measures which I employed: above all, demonstrating that [(a)] the received view is absolutely untenable. And [(b)] that it would be impossible, at any rate, to give a difference between the state of believing and that of presenting without believing, if there were not a second, fundamentally different manner of relating.

(2) That the power of the 'is' in existential propositions is identical to the one of the copula.

The received view claims the opposite; one is so proud of having found the equivocation.

Even if one demonstrates that the judgment 'some tree is' is the same as the judgment 'there is a tree', or, that 'some tree is green' = 'there is a green tree', one fails to trust [oneself] and, for the longest period of time, suspends one's judgment. One does not notice, indeed one denies again and again, what seems to be so readily noticeable.

24. Deceptions by linguistic expressions are prejudices based on habit which in particular need to be identified.[17] It is curious how often they have prevented important scientists from noticing relatively simple things.

(1) If language uses the same expression, one suspects, by force of habit, that the same process is expressed. This is why HOBBES came to believe that, because the 'is' of the affirmative copula appears also in the expression of the negative ones, only with an added 'not', the affirmative copula are also present in this case, [and thus] that all negative judgments are affirmative, only with a different matter. Hence he failed to see the whole difference between the way of relating in affirming and that in negating. ⎫

41⎪42

Yet SIGWART[17a] still takes exception to the so-called negative copula's supposedly being more compound than the affirmative one. And, having been confused by this, he does not wish to admit, and hence *de facto* is unable to notice, that in denying there is a relation which is opposed, but nevertheless as simple as the relation in believing.

(2) [Another deception by linguistic expressions is given in the belief] that the logical O is negative and that consequently the logical A is affirmative. (Possibly even stronger: everything and nothing appear as opposites; hence where language uses 'everything', it appears to express a positive, affirmative judgment.) Refutation by means of the existential proposition [*Existenzialsatz*]. Prior to such a refutation, [many people are] virtually intransigent if one points out that this sentence is positive and that one negative. They do not notice anything of the involved way of relating, because they erroneously believe in the presence of the opposite one.

(3) Just recently, in a seminar, I have come across this in the context of A is A. Despite all the explanations, I received letters referring to inner perception, where, as a matter of fact, the correct state of affairs was not noticed because of the prejudices arising from linguistic expressions (and presumably also because of habitually rooted direct (special) prejudices).

(4) Indeed, language often creates a prejudice detrimental to noticing because it lacks a name for a certain fact, like, for example, for

the analogue of evidence in certain emotional activities [*Gemüts-tätigkeiten*].

25. It is likewise possible to trace back to force of habit the prejudices of [certain] researchers (who [themselves] are not in-experienced in noticing) which prevent them from noticing that black is a positive colour-phenomenon, or, for that matter, that it is a positive phenomenon at all. Or, [which prevent them from noticing] that violet contains red and blue, and that orange contains red and yellow, and thus that they both are mixed phenomena [*Misch-phänomene*].

Diverse influences tend to give rise to diverse phenomena; for example, a prick in the finger and a pressure on the shoulder; [each] one [of the influences gives rise] to one of the phenomena.

Having become used to accepting this as being generally the case, these researchers are opposed to taking violet and orange as double-phenomena, because they are induced by simple sensory waves 42!43 [*Sinneswellen*] ¦ of a certain [single] wavelength, [i.e.] by simple light [as occurring] in the decomposition of light rays in a prism. FICK[17b] (in connection with the YOUNG-HELMHOLTZ hypothesis[17c]) prefered to take yellow to be red-green than violet to be red-blue. In contrast, HELMHOLTZ himself, while declaring violet to be a simple phenomenon, has shown on one occasion that he had a good mind to regard white as being phenomenally composed of many colours. It is just that not everyone was able to discern them analytically in the way he did. (Popular Lectures.)[18]

26. We can already see how, in many cases, prejudices based on habit can get in the way of noticing the facts as they are.

And yet, we have so far touched upon relatively few things. Every error which arises from an overhasty induction, actually stems from an inclination based on habit, because this inclination drives one to judge whatever is new in the old established way.

HERBART's[18a] belief that the validity of categorical judgments is only hypothetical, and that, even if they are affirmative, they never include a concomitant affirmation of the subject, is an example of a confusion of the sort discussed here. He found that this did hold for many [categorical judgments] which he thought were affirmative. (KANT seems to have preceded him in this, [see KANT's] error [concerning the] ontological argument).[19] So he was led to believe that this is the case for all of them.

45

Thus: Cassius has died,
Brutus lives – only hypothetically, no concomitant affirmation of the subject!

Curious indeed that a thinker like HERBART does not notice the true nature of the act! That he does not notice what appears to be so easily noticeable! And that many of his students even nowadays hold the same erroneous doctrine [*Irrlehre*].

27. It might, however, be possible that it was not simply an incomplete induction creating the prejudice in HERBART which led him astray in such a striking way.

Maybe, the genesis is something more complicated:

(a) The finding in all general so-called affirmative judgments.
(b) The belief that the general includes the particular.
(c) From this the conclusion, that no affirmative judgment could be other than hypothetical, i.e. that there is no concomitant affirmation of the subject.

43¦44   The same would then, of course, hold for categorical ¦ judgments in general. HERBART was indeed the sort of person who would trust deduction over even the most forceful appearances. (After all, was it not he who, for the sake of deduction, declared motion, becoming and the I as not really existing.)

And thus his consent to what practically every unprejudiced person would notice most easily was inhibited by deduction.

The ultimate roots [of his prejudices] were previous errors, in particular about the affirmative character of 'A' judgments.

And so, these roots can again be traced back to the misleading influence of habits which we have demonstrated earlier.

28. At any rate, even though habit is the source of many prejudices, it is not responsible for all of them. Many prejudices arise partially or completely from different sources.

(a) The instinctive urge to judge immediately; indeed even in cases where no habit [is involved] – like outer perception, [or] memory.
(b) Furthermore, it is tempting to rush into judgments because of the tiring and slow nature of cumbersome precautionary measures.

Judgments which have been formed in this manner have often proved to be a remarkable hindrance to noticing what is relatively easy to notice.

Example: LANGE's[19a] account of his experiments concerning the blind spot. [He claims that] after some period of contest [between two colours] he does not see anything in the place of the blind spot. And that the [visual] sense, having obviously overturned its false conclusion, becomes clear that there is as little colour in the blind spot as there is [in those places located] towards the back [of the head[19b]].

This claim [is] decidedly wrong. Filling in by the other visual field. My experiment with the after-image [*Nachbild*]. LANGE thus just didn't notice; why not? It was inconceivable to him that there is a colour different from the two competing ones. That one he didn't see. So he was convinced that there was no colour present, and didn't notice anything of what should have been so easy to notice.

Others, who are predisposed to find it unbelievable that a colour phenomenon could occur in a place where there is no [corresponding] sensitive region on the retina – and who again ignore the fact that the other eye is supplementing, due to the identity of the regions 44|45 – have even claimed that in fact there never is a filling in ¦ of the blind spot. They are not lying, yet what they claim is certainly false, hence our only conclusion can be that this filling in was never noticed by them.

Amongst them are men (scientists) who otherwise have proven to be competent observers, and who are also practised in psychological analysis: so powerful has been the impediment to noticing arising through overhasty prejudice in this context.

29. A contrary conviction is a hindrance, indeed even a predominant contrary opinion will have the same effect. One does not like to dwell on convincing oneself through precise examination whether something, which one is fairly certain in denying, might not be present after all.

30. In contrast, a correct conjecture, or a conviction (drawn from some other source) that a certain fact [*Tatsache*] is indeed given in consciousness, has undoubtably in many cases been helpful in noticing.

[Given such a conjecture or conviction] one will obviously be inclined to get a confirmation through direct observation. Like an astronomer, having calculated the position of a star, or the onset of an eclipse.

To get such a conviction from some other source will often have an extraordinary preparatory effect.

(For example, in the relationship of judgment or in the consequences of evidence; [see also] HELMHOLTZ's picking out [*Heraushören*] of overtones [in his investigation of] tone colours.)[19c]

Admittedly, it can happen (in singular cases) that someone deludes himself by imagining that he is noticing without actually doing so. After all, many people have claimed to have noticed what was not present at all, or what may have been present but which could not have been noticed by them or, for that matter, by anyone else.

But [I shall talk] of how this can happen later.

31. We have just discussed the elimination of prejudices against (and the creation of a conjecture favourable to) the fact which is to be noticed.

In this context, we must also add a few words about the creation of goodwill, a topic which is closely connected to what we have just talked about.

45/46   Many people take a certain theoretical dislike to a ¦ fact which is meant to be noticed. Because this fact does not fit their hypotheses, they wish it would not exist. Such wishes do not have the power to eliminate the facts, but they can make it less easy to notice them.

32. The history of science contains curious spectacles. The Royal Society and LEIBNIZ, NEWTON himself and HUYGHENS, BILLROTH[19d] and PASTEUR and KOCH.[19e]

People [with the above mentioned sort of dislike] would be incomparably better disposed [to noticing] if one could completely purify their theoretical interest. Or, if one could show to them that the fact in question has theoretically desirable consequences, as well as the undesirable ones. Or, if it were possible at the outset to diminish the value they attach to the erroneous hypotheses due to which they are disinclined to see the fact in question. I believe to have found cases where important researchers, who otherwise have proven to be impartial, have been crucially hampered by this as far as psychognostic questions are concerned.

(a) It is, for example, striking that, in the case of the question as to

48

whether the result of mixing certain colours (monocular or binocular, directly or by means of after-images, or however else) has a tinge of this or that colour, researchers usually claim to notice or, [for that matter] not to notice, according to whichever would be more favourable to their hypotheses.

(b) Fear of MEINONG's relapse concerning evidence.[20]

33. Apart from goodwill, one might, in the absence of theoretical resistance, furthermore wish to mention the arousal of energetic enthusiasm to notice, [or] the arousal of hope and courage to notice. (But this without animated passions. NEWTON, who is unable to carry out the calculations which demonstrate that, according to the new data, his hypotheses coincide exactly with the facts.)

Many a one [believes]: 'Nothing can be determined. One [person] says this, another one that, one believes this fundamental taxonomy [*Grundeinteilung*] to be true, the other another one.'

This [attitude] frustrates a serious approach and a patient preparation. It seems to me the time has come [for a change,] and [with it the prospect of] rich gains.# |

46¦47

34. [It is,] on the other hand [clear that] an incentive to making an effort can be gained not just by emphasizing the importance [of the task] but also [by emphasizing] the difficulty [of it].

Because thoughtlessness [*Leichtsinn*] provides as little incentive to taking all the [required] care as does despair. (How difficult the progress of natural science was in every discovery.)

But in this case [one also finds] aversion! For here, more often than in other domains, we find that essential things, which had been found, have been completely lost again.

35. Yet another precondition, belonging to the less immediate factors [involved in bringing about noticing]*, which is important as a means to success, must be mentioned. It is to try to win time for noticing.

If the duration of a phenomenon is short, then all kinds of preparations must be readied in advance. This is

(a) because such preparations cost time, [and]

[See] my paper: '*Über die Gründe der Entmutigung auf philosophischem Gebiete*'.[21]
* See pp. 40–3.

49

(b) because noticing may take time.

(1) Every psychical function requires a certain time to come into being. Like, for example, the change of psychical states, [or] the thought of a temporal sequence [*Gedanke eines zeitlichen Verlaufs*]. (However, it might be possible that noticing arises simultaneously with the phenomenon; in the way in which the perception of the totality of actual consciousness [is created simultaneously] with it.)

[It is] questionable whether [this is] true in every sense. How is one to conceive of the genesis of an immediate axiom, or of an insight [*Einsicht*] into a conclusion? [Through] a gradual growth of intensity? [This would be an] erroneous view.

(2) Many [instances of] noticing appear to (include or) presuppose other [instances of] noticing.

For example, the noticing of a pervading part [includes or presupposes] the noticing of the concretum containing this part, and the noticing of a logical part (the generic determination) [includes or presupposes] the noticing of the logical whole in question.

47|48

Reservation: 'The difference in [the case of] violet [might possibly be] muddled, ¦ indeed lightness and place [might be] mixed in, as in the case of sounds. But then the same [would presumably hold] for the genus'.

However, in this case it might also be that one [instance of] noticing [*das eine Bemerken*] sometimes takes place simultaneously with another one.

(Similar to the following cases of simultaneous occurrence: pleasure or disgust about a certain sensory quality together with that quality; a judgment together with the idea [*Vorstellung*] upon which it is based, and, indeed, inner perception together with the presentation [*Vorstellung*] and the object.)

(3) Of several sounds we tend to take the louder one for the earlier one. This could be explained in the following way: [the louder tones] take a shorter [period of] time to be noticed; hence [we could conclude that] each of [the involved instances of] noticing occurs only some time after the occurrence of what is to be noticed. Yet it might also be sufficient [for an explanation] to assume that these periods of time and their difference are [only] necessary to 'take note' and to determine.

36. *Nota bene*: It is, in general, undeniable that one can notice without determining [what is noticed]. Because of this, we have

50

in many cases difficulties in many in knowing whether we did not notice, or whether we merely did not determine. For it is impossible to determine whether this or that is being noticed, without determining what is noticed.

But then this sort of noticing* cannot be used for psychognostic purposes, which means that the above-mentioned difficulties are quite irrelevant for us.

37. And I would reply in the same way to someone who objects that many of the things which I identified as obstacles for noticing may indeed only be obstacles for determining. ([A claim] which may neither be refutable nor demonstrable.) This may well be the case, but it is quite irrelevant for our practical purposes.

38. Finally, another item which is to be counted amongst the less immediate preparations. It is advantageous if a person who is meant to notice some object that is difficult to notice has previously been acquainted, at least in a general manner, with this object. Say, if, in another context, he is able to notice more easily something which is the same, or very similar to this object, like, for example, a sound, [or] the tone colour of an instrument.

48|49

Someone will more easily notice evidence if he knows the peculiar feature in a general way than if he notices it for the first time. The noticing of an emotion [Gemütsbewegung], which is characterized as being correct, is supported by a previous noticing of the analogue to evidence.

Di-energy [Dienergie].[21a] [It is] sometimes more easily noticeable than usual. MILL notices it only in the phenomena of memory, [and he does so] because of the difference of times [in noticing] which creates a particular contrast between the one and the other correlate. I have often used this with success in order to make it noticeable in other contexts.

39. We have thus listed the main factors concerning the less immediate kinds of preparations for bringing others to notice [something] in difficult cases.

Let us now identify those factors which need to be considered in order to bring someone to notice who has been sufficiently prepared.

---

* I take it that Brentano refers here to noticing without determining.

40. We can distinguish two kinds of means. The first one is to bring him [the person who is sufficiently prepared] to make certain comparisons. The second one is to arouse something in his consciousness which, through the laws of association, might be adequate to bring about his noticing.

41. [Let us] first [discuss] comparisons. What I have in mind here is best explained by a few examples.[21b]

(a) Let us assume that I have a colour in front of me which comes close to pure blue, yet which still displays a certain red tinge. And, assuming I wish to get someone to notice this peculiarity who has not as yet done so, then I might be able to achieve my aim by proceeding in the following way: I show him a pure, and shall we say, equally saturated [and] strongly illuminated blue, [then I] exchange it with the reddish one and ask him to compare the impressions. In many cases, he will then recognize the difference with ease, and he will notice that the source of this difference is exclusively given in the reddishness of the second impression.

(b) Another method which may immediately make the difference apparent to him is to have both colours adjacent to ¦ one another and to let their border pass through the region of clearest vision. The difference will then be noticed by him (reddish).

49¦50

This method appears to be less recommendable, but only because of a coincidental circumstance.

[Namely, when we are dealing with a] simultaneous contrast, in that the phenomena are changed on both sides. This means that reddishness is not actually noticed in the preceding phenomenon, but in another one.

Yet, if the colours succeed one another immediately, then one will notice the reddishness there also successively. Indeed, even though the simultaneous [contrast] is strongest in the first instance, the successive one will, over time, become stronger and stronger.

One needs to look longer!

Then, simultaneous light-induction [*Lichtinduktion*] will start.

[Objection:] far from being an impediment, simultaneous contrast even aids noticing. Because blue is something different from reddish blue. This difference adds itself to the one given originally and thus makes it easier to recognize [*erkennen*]. For if it wasn't for an originally existing difference, there would not be a simultaneous contrast.

Answer: In that case we are dealing with the drawing of a conclusion which is not an [instance of] noticing. Even though the conclusion that [something is] present would be correct, the conclusion that [something is] noticed would be false.

Accordingly, simultaneous contrast [is] undeniably a disturbance. Apart from it, one could say that [the presently discussed] manner of comparing is perfectly adequate.

Indeed, [if it were possible to disregard this disturbance, then] the [present] method of comparison would essentially be the same [as the one looked at previously].

In both cases we had several phenomena being compared. At first, they are noticed as a whole. [Yet] some of them are different from others because they contain a part which the others don't, and thus the part is noticed.

50:51 Looking a bit more closely, the process of the ¦ second method appears, however, somewhat more intricate than I have just described it.

The two colour phenomena which I have side by side are not only different because the one is reddish and the other is not, but also because they are differently localized.

It would be better for the inducement of noticing the reddishness if this second reason for difference did not exist.

However, these ills are at least mitigated by the fact that [the difference of localization can be made] to approach the unnoticeable (the infinitesimal) and by the fact that there are the same or bigger differences in the spatial determination without the difference given by reddishness.

Yet the only way to overcome these ills completely is to repeat the experiment several times by exchanging the positions of what has been put side by side in each repetition. By doing this one incorporates the method of succession.

We thus have an intricate method of comparison which brings out part agreements, part differences.

Nota bene: The same kind of intricacy can actually also be found in the initially mentioned method of comparison. For, on closer inspection [of this method], one also finds several reasons for difference:

The reddishness,

53

the difference of the times in intuiting [*die Zeitdifferenz in der Anschauung*],

because one of the phenomena may be a phenomenon of memory (phenomenon of original association) [while the other isn't], or, if both are [phenomena of memory], because one modifies more than the other.

And here again [there are] mitigations:

for one, the [possibility of] infinitesimal temporal difference [between the two phenomena],

for another the existence of the same or bigger time differences without the difference of reddishness.

The obstacle will be made even less conspicuous by repeating the experiment in reverse temporal order.

(c) A method of comparison very similar to this will achieve the aim in many other cases. ¦

51¦52

In order to get someone to notice the peculiarity of evidence which distinguishes certain judgments from others as being blind ones, we put together, for example, evident and blind judgments [*blinde Urteile*]. The judgments [–] which do or do not contain evidence as one of their pervading parts [–] are first of all noticed as a whole; their difference is noticed and finally the grounds for this difference is found to lie in the possession or the lack of the characteristic [meant] to be noticed.

But in this case it is even more important than in the previous ones that one does not content oneself with having a single evident judgment compared with a single non-evident one, [especially] if one wants to be as certain of success as possible. Because two such judgments might display many other, considerable differences. [They might be]

directed upon different objects,

possibly apodeictic – not apodeictic,

possibly affirmative – negative,

possibly adopted as the immediate consequence of a different assumption.

The difference is thus only partially rooted in the possession or lack of evidence, and thus does not explicitly indicate either. Rather it does so only in a very implicit (confused) manner.

The indication only becomes explicit through a composite method of comparison. [Namely, a method] which makes the particular concomitant differences [*Mitdifferenzen*] harmless by constantly retaining the peculiarity of the difference of evidence under all the variations of the material, modal and qualitative factors, as well as [under all the variations] of the factor of immediacy or dependency of judgments, and of whatever else might be contributory.

(d) Something very similar is true of getting [someone] to notice modality, that is the apodeictic character which certain judgments possess, and others lack.

(e) In these examples we were dealing with a kind of privative* contrast; a positive factor was only on one side; on the other was the lack of it.

In other cases, where we are dealing with a positive contrast, the method will nevertheless, [at least] in essence, remain the

same. ¦

And the two differentiating positive factors will again become noticeable, as was the case for the positive and the lack of it. – Whether this will be easier or more difficult will depend on the particular circumstances. One of the more important of these circumstances will be immediately clear given what has been said so far: the amount of diversity of the comparative processes which is required.

(f) For example, a very simple case is where the affirmative quality of some judgment [say, A_1] becomes noticeable through contrasting it with a negative judgment [say, N_1], assuming that they [A_1 and N_1] are without difference [as concerns] matter etc.

The two qualities are [in this case] noticed simultaneously. And with this the noticing of quality in general is given, or, at least, [it is] made very easy [in the following way].

If we put the two judgments which differ [only] with respect to quality [i.e. A_1 and N_1] together with two others [say, A_2 and N_2] which [themselves] differ in [at least] some other respect, but concur as concerns quality with the one or the other [i.e. with A_1, or N_1], then it will be immediately clear that the two affirmative ones [A_1 and A_2] differ in another way than either of the affirmative judgments [i.e. A_1 or A_2] differs from the respective negative one [i.e. N_1 or N_2 respectively]. Indeed, the positive contrast [Gegensatz], like the privative one, reveals itself immediately in the moment the two contrasts are simultaneously noticed. And there is no contrast without unity of genus [Gattung].[21c]

* privative (adj.) expressing absence or negation [Chambers].

Nota bene: It is not yet the time to speak of the relation of contrast. For the moment let me just say that it is not always the case that a positive contrast is given by a difference where positive distinguishing factors are on both sides.

Consider, for example, the following case: a blind judgment like 'There must be a three-dimensional space', is made apodeictically, while an evident one (like 'I think, [therefore] I am') is made only assertorically. In this case, there are positive distinguishing factors on both sides, since the first judgment is apodeictic and the second one evident. But this does not mean that we have a positive contrast rather than two privative ones. [To be] evident and [to be] apodeictic thus are not mutually

53¦54   exclusive, and they do not belong to one ¦ genus, but they determine the complex [*Kompositum*] of mutually pervading parts in completely different respects.

The situation is completely different in the case of affirmative and negative quality which we have just talked about.

(g) It would, of course, be possible to multiply indefinitely the examples which I have just given to illustrate the method of comparison, [i.e.] that peculiar combination of differences which makes explicitly noticeable what has been implicitly perceived.

In the domain of colours, it is not only possible, as we have seen earlier, to make a previously unnoticed red tinge noticeable by means of comparison, but the differences of light and dark, and the difference between the genus of lightness and that of the quality of colours [*Gattung der Farbenqualität*] can be made noticeable in the same manner.

(h) In the domain of sound, the difference between loud and quiet, and with it the particularity of the genus of intensity as opposed to other sides of the tone-phenomenon, will noticeably come to the fore in sound-phenomena which are the same in all other respects.

The difference of the pitch [*Tonhelligkeit, Tonhöhe*] as opposed to the quality of sound in the narrow sense will become noticeable in the same way if the note C is compared with C, middle C and high C. [The same difference will also become noticeable] if, *vice versa*, it is shown that a sound, which itself cannot be dissolved into notes of the scale, has a pitch equal to a certain note on the continuous scale, by demonstrating that the sound is higher than some note [on the scale] and lower than some other, and thus showing that the sound must coincide in

56

pitch with some point [on the continuous scale] and yet be qualitatively different from it.

42. Enough examples. To give any more would not in any essential way further the understanding of what I had in mind when I said that the method in which we brought someone to notice explicitly something implicitly given was to bring him to make comparisons adequate for that purpose.

43. Thinking of the processes through which we first had been led to notice explicitly certain particular parts in the complex of our consciousness, [that is to say, the sort of] processes which in the psychical life of any mature individual would have to be referred 54¦55 to as being prehistoric, ¦ we can, in my view, confidently claim that they must have consisted in such comparisons.

Of course, these differences were not deliberately put together in an artificial manner. They combined on their own. [This happened] through partial changes which were induced in otherwise persisting states of consciousness [*Bewusstseinslage*] by new impressions, like, for example, in a novel stimulation of a sense or of a part of a sensory field. A difference emerged immediately, and the source of this difference, be it the finding of something positive on both sides or on one side only, lifted itself into relatively explicit consciousness. In the course of this, consciousness itself might have contained a great multitude of further differentiated elements. It was hence the partial change against the background of a complete or, at least, approximate stillness of other parts which initially brought into this chaos the light that led us to a differentiation of special components [*besondere Momente*].

The first [instance of] noticing was then followed in quick succession by another and yet another [instance of] noticing. [This happened] partly because of a similar spontaneous combination of differences, partly favoured by the desire to notice, which, according to what we have said before, is raised by what is new [or] by what is striking because it breaks a habit [or] by what is astonishing. The infant, barely woken up to life, looks at the world full of amazement and every look, so to speak, is a question. When this sort of theoretical desire is tied to a part which has been noticed, it can sometimes happen that all other processes are left out of consideration. The differences in the more narrow domain [i.e. the part which has been noticed] then appear as if they were alone and so

57

lead to an analysis which penetrates into finer and finer parts. And thus, the class of what is noticeable and actually noticed grows like an avalanche. We are adding to it, sometimes without, sometimes with a certain deliberateness [*Absichtlichkeit*], before we have any thought of advancing to the final elements of consciousness, [or] of constructing a psychognosy. Already at that time comparison was the essential vehicle for progress. This should be sufficient to demonstrate the great importance of this factor. |

55:56

44. All that remains to be done is to explain the way in which association can be used to lead [someone] to notice [something].

45. You will all have heard of [the] association of ideas and its laws. You might also have found that psychologists differ in the way they define them.

Some people have put forward a law of similarity [*Gesetz der Ähnlichkeit*], a law of contiguity [*G. der Kontiguität*], a law of contrast [*G. des Kontrastes*] and the like. Others have disputed the one or the other, for example, the law of contrast. Many (like, for example, J.S. MILL) also spoke of a law of association of the same with the same [*desselben an dasselbe*], and believed that this is always involved in associations through contiguity.

46. If one asks 'What is associated?', many believe that it is only presentations [*Vorstellungen*] of [i.e. which have] the character of experiences. If the experiences in question had been had at an earlier time, then they would recur later, only usually in a weakened form.

47. But this is completely wrong. Even though there might well be [associations of] this [sort]: [say,] in a dream or in a fever. Johannes MÜLLER[21d] has correctly pointed out that it is not just presentations of the character of experiences but also concepts which are associated.

We associate an idea [*Vorstellung*] with the name 'colour', or the name '5' etc., which is a concept [and as such] differs in kind [*ist heterogen*] from experiences.

48. For similar reasons, none of the other current theories is flawless. Certain incorrect determinations are adopted. So, for example, the law of association of the same with the same [adopted by] J.S. MILL and, if I remember correctly, even before him by HAMILTON.[21e] This

58

law would have to be understood [in the sense of] the same being mutually associated both conceptually and in concrete intuition [*in konkreter Anschauung*]. But this is not MILL's view; he does not believe in general concepts, he only knows general names. He misinterprets the peculiar impression we have if something appears familiar to us.

And [yet], in other respects, the determinations [adopted] have turned out to be too narrow. They do not include the cases where we connect ideas [*Ideen*] which were [previously] never connected by us, but which are being connected only ¦ because analogous ties were established by us earlier, say, in a joke.

56¦57

49. The person who has spoken most aptly about the association of ideas was, without doubt, ARISTOTLE. He subsumed it under the general feature habit [*allgemeine Tatsache der Gewohnheit*], which asserts itself not just in the domain of presentation [*Vorstellung*], but with reference to all forms of psychical behaviour.

Certain activities leave behind certain dispositions to act similarly under similar circumstances. This is what we mean when we say that one gets into the habit of [doing] something. As far as this getting into the habit is concerned, we only need to distinguish two kinds of laws[: (a)] the ones referring to the grounds and the continued existence of the disposition, [and (b)] the ones referring to the activity [of the disposition]:

ad (a) Repeated acts [of the] same or [a] similar [kind] reinforce the disposition of the habit. Yet, it might also happen that a single (energetic) act which stands out is sufficient to bring about a strong habit (ARISTOTLE).

Opposing acts, indeed the mere lack of practice, lead to a weakening of the disposition, indeed, possibly, to a complete loss.

So we speak of fresh memory etc.

ad (b) The more the new circumstances are like the old ones in all the essential respects, the more perfect will be the activity of the disposition. [Say,] I had had a thought, at some earlier time, which I connected with a multitude of other factors (say by weaving it into some plan). It will then be in many ways very advantageous for a revival [*Wiedererweckung*] of this thought, should these other factors all find themselves again in my consciousness.

50. Turning from these general remarks about association to our [particular] case, it is probably immediately clear how associations can lead to something being noticed,

57¦58

(a) As in the case of any other activity, it is also possible to create a habit advantageous to noticing. ¦

(b) If we present to ourselves explicitly, and not just implicitly, a particular part of a presented whole, then presumably we will always notice this explicit presenting. Now, if the explicit presentation is associated with something in such a way that the presentation is aroused [erweckt] by it, then an [instance of] noticing will concomitantly arise.

(c) Concepts are gained out of concrete intuitions, and if, at some later stage, we think them again, then they will always have concrete intuition as their foundation. If, in some case or other, we are given a concrete presentation, in fact [if we are given] an object with which we were attentively occupied, and if a concept is recalled by some means given through the association of ideas, then it is likely that the said presentation is being used as foundation [for this concept], and that thus the corresponding feature [i.e. the feature corresponding to the concept] in the presentation is noticed. Or, if this should not have happened immediately, then it is probable that it will happen at least at some later time.

51. What we have said about the influences of habit on noticing is confirmed by facts.

(a) If someone is in the habit of paying attention [achten auf] to a certain thing, then he will notice it immediately and at first glance, whereas someone else would possibly have found it only later.

(b) We have said that a habit can often be momentarily particularly strong because of its recent formation [die Frische der Begründung]. And so we find, for example, that if someone, of whom one spoke just moments earlier, is passing by, then he is more likely to be noticed than otherwise.

Or, if a moment ago, the conversation had been of a coin, and if, by coincidence, there was one lying on the road in front of me, then I would notice it more easily than otherwise.

60

(c) Consider what we are doing when we are looking for something. We keep the conceptual presentation which we have of [what we are looking for] continuously present [in our minds], and if the thing or something similar somehow turns up somewhere, we will be struck by it and we will notice what otherwise we would not have noticed. ⁞

58⁞59

(d) The way in which association supports noticing is particularly exhibited in the so-called presentations of fantasy [*Phantasievorstellungen*], like, if you wish, the sounds which we present to ourselves by means of the power of our imagination when inventing or repeating some melody in our mind. We are dealing here with weak sound experiences, created in a subjective manner. They are so weak that, no matter how weak a sound we create vocally, it will make a louder impression than the loudest sound which we only fantasize. Some people thus refuse to believe that actual sounds occur in fantasy, for they think that phenomena of such a weak nature could not be noticed.

Nevertheless, they are [actual] and they mix in peculiar ways with the noises coming from outside: rattling of cars, the rhythmic beat of rail joints. If we notice them but would not (or only with great difficulty) notice equally weak sounds, then we must no doubt put this [instance of] noticing down to the facilitating influence of the association to which they owe their genesis.

52. The simplest way of using association to let someone notice something is to identify it by description [*namhaft machen*].

53. The more precisely we do this, the more likely it is to be crowned with success. Even if we cannot do it precisely, we will achieve considerable results if, by determining a more narrow domain, we focus the attention on what is most closely related or adjacent. In doing so, the attention will more easily succeed in arriving at the ultimate goal by the previously mentioned method of comparisons.

54. But, since linguistic associations are not the only ones, it is obvious that it can be useful to arouse other [items] which are connected with this and similar [types of] noticing by some habitual connection [*Gewohnheitsbeziehung*].

61

55. In making someone pay attention through naming, it is often also the case that what is immediately associated with the name is different in content from what is meant to be noticed. Even though the two are convertible, it is only this immediate association of the name to which ¦ the thing to be noticed associates itself in its proper presentation [*eigentliche Vorstellung*]. This will become clearer in the discussion on 'determining' ['*Bestimmen*'] which is to follow shortly.

59¦60

56. And since one associative factor (associative clue) might collaborate with another one according to the laws of habit, it may, in difficult cases, be useful to provide stimuli from different sides.

This does not lead to a distracting proliferation, but rather to a more perfect focusing of the view on the point towards which, so to speak, all the radii converge.

57. So, one clearly cannot deny the importance of the associative factor. All the same, the comparisons of which we have spoken earlier remain by far the more crucial means (without them, one would not even have come to notice particular components in the confused complex of our consciousness).

58. This is the small bit of knowledge which we have of the laws governing the occurrence of noticing. It is essentially given in the way in which we use these laws in solving psychognostic problems.

59. If we want to achieve this [problem solving] with greatest possible completeness, then naturally we must proceed in an ordered manner. We will divide consciousness into different branches, [and] get to work on them sequentially, one after another. We will look across the border [of the branch under investigation] only in order to bring in factors useful for the comparisons and the analogies which are so important to us. In concentrating the attention upon a single part, further parts will become noticeable in it. And thus the process of order and of concentration which successively passes through the sequence, is reiterated until the indivisible elements are reached.

60. But, will this method, carried out with all care, really always be crowned with success? Or will there not be cases where, in spite of all our efforts, noticing will fail?

60¦61   Unfortunately, the latter is undoubtedly [the case]. ¦

61. The cases where noticing *fails* despite taking all possible care can be divided into four classes.

The first is the one where the factors which we mentioned as immediate means for noticing are simply inapplicable.

In this context, we must particularly look at the principle of comparison [*Prinzip der Vergleichung*] because the auxiliary means [provided through] association can only be put into action if, at some previous time, the principle of comparison has led to the same, or, (wherever it may be sufficient) at least, to a very similar [type of] noticing. Noticing, as we described it, presupposes, however, that we encounter in our consciousness privative or positive contrasts to what we are meant to notice. But this cannot *a priori* be expected to happen in each and every case. What should prevent there being a certain element which exists generally in the phenomena of our consciousness, in the sense that each of them participates in it and is penetrated by it as one pervading part penetrates another one? Should this be the case, then it will be absolutely impossible to notice this part explicitly.

One might object that this danger appears to be out of the question because we actually do possess intuitive presentations [*anschauliche Vorstellungen*] with contents which have nothing at all in common, like the so-called physical phenomena in contrast to the psychical ones. Physical phenomena do not contain anything but quality in a certain lightness and intensity, and the individuating factor of the spatial determination [*örtliche Bestimmtheit*]. Psychical phenomena, in contrast, possess nothing of this, except in a very loose way. These privative contrasts are used to distinguish the psychical which is currently in the content of our consciousness from these so-called physical phenomena, and to make them noticeable as something special. But they are insufficient for a further analysis of the parts of the psychical. The only useful auxiliary means for this purpose are the privative contrasts in presenting, judging, willing, etc. Now, if these [auxiliary means] constantly had some immutable element in common, then it would be impossible to make a comparison which 61|62 would lead us ¦ to notice it. We would have to abandon without hope any experiments [to that effect].

I have already mentioned that we have reasons to believe that there actually is such an unnoticeable part in us. We do not understand ourselves as [given] in an abstract concept, but as [given] in a concrete, individual intuition, and yet we are incapable of giving an account of the individuating factor.

63

This state of affairs would change immediately if we were given access to some other inner life.

So much of the first [of the four classes].

62. A second class of cases can be found where we are dealing with magnitudes which are capable of continuous increase and decrease. For it turns out in this context that noticing becomes more difficult as the magnitude decreases. Indeed, that it simply becomes impossible to notice anything which in magnitude falls below a certain limit. This is manifest

(a) in the case of spatial magnitudes, [or] spatial thresholds; [and]

(b) in the case of intensity – in whatever way one might understand its nature. Phenomena of very weak intensity will be less easily noticed, [while] those with an altogether too weak intensity will not be noticeable at all. Intensity-threshold.

(c) The same is true in the case of qualitative factors like a red tinge etc. – whatever one may initially think of their nature. Again, the weaker the factor, the more easily it will be overlooked. If [the factor] is too weak, [it is] unnoticeable.

(d) We said earlier that psychical phenomena do not have spatial magnitudes. Yet [they possess] an analogous composition [*Zusammensetzung*] of continuously connected parts. The space which is seen, e.g., corresponds piece by piece to a part of the seeing [*Teil des Sehens*]. Again, it is possible to speak of bigger and smaller parts in this context. The smaller ones will be less or not at all noticeable. Indeed, the limit of noticeability will correspond to the limit associated with the space which is seen.

62|63   (e) The same is true with respect to dimness [*Schwäche*]. |

(f) And [it is true] of the qualitative factors which I mentioned before.

Yet another difficulty and barrier for noticing is given in the case of those magnitudes which can decrease and increase continuously.

As mentioned before, in order to notice, we require the comparison of different things [*Vergleichung von Differentem*]. In the case we are considering now, these differences will be magnitudes. This is not so elsewhere, say, for example, [in the case of]

the difference between affirmation and negation,

the difference between evident and blind,

the difference between psychical and physical phenomena,
the difference between colour and tone.

[In the present case we are dealing with] continuous magnitudes with infinitely many infinitely small parts.

Will the difference in magnitude of the differences be irrelevant? Or will it be that bigger magnitudes serve us better, while the very small ones will not serve us at all? Obviously, we expect the latter to be the case and, indeed, this expectation is met by experience.

Thus, very small differences are insufficient for the requirements of noticing. (It may be that this is the case for differences in intensity in the domain of colours, if indeed there are any such differences at all.) This is why intensity in colours is denied [even] by excellent scientists. But without justification. Comparison with other sensory domains is helpful. Indeed, it shows that there is always a high intensity present.

Time, too, is a continuous magnitude. And the difficulty in noticing very short phenomena, which has been mentioned before, is connected with this continuity. If the duration of a phenomenon falls below a certain limit, then it becomes simply unnoticeable. This is why we can count this case also as being amongst those of the second class.

63. A third class of cases where something is unnoticeable is the one which includes those cases where something is unnoticeable because of inescapable disturbances of attention during the analysis. We count amongst [these disturbances] :

63|64

(a) phenomena of extreme fatigue,
(b) phenomena of extreme excitement, of raging anger, etc.,
(c) phenomena where, regardless of how little excitement they might involve, attention is nevertheless absorbed and therefore not free for psychognostic analysis. For example, mathematical calculations etc. [or] distracting complications. Surrogate: the study within memory.

64. A fourth class, finally, is formed by the cases of individual insurmountable incompetence, [as given by, say,]

(a) congenital lack of talent,
(b) (possibly) acquired incompetence.

If it should be true that the habit not to notice something can be developed, in certain cases, to such an extent that it becomes second nature and wholly ineradicable, then this would be a case belonging to this fourth class. HELMHOLTZ, for example, believed that this is so.

Indeed, quite apart from the experiences which HELMHOLTZ believes he is able to provide, one could also argue deductively in favour of this point of view, provided it is acceptable that a temporary complete incompetence in noticing is formed in this manner.

How should the competence [*Fähigkeit*] [to notice] be regained, given that each new attempt leads to a [new instance of] not-noticing, and thus to a stronger habit in not-noticing?

It seems that help could only be found in time – [i.e. in] a long abstinence in making attempts. But an abstinence of this duration is not acceptable in all cases. (All the same, the argument may not be as stringent as it seems.) Even if in the new attempts to pay attention noticing is not achieved, it may still be possible to have triumphed over the unfavourable habit in some respects because paying attention is a complicated process. Progressing from [these partial triumphs] one might ultimately even completely regain the lost competence. What therefore appears as essential are only the experiences (H[ELMHOLTZ], too, puts great emphasis on this point). –

64|65 Whether it is true for all people that they [i.e. the experiences] ¦ in certain respects give rise, through habituation [*durch Gewöhnung*], to an incompetence which is virtually invincible [is an issue which,] for the moment, shall not be investigated. It is certainly the case for some people. Amongst the invincible obstacles created through habit are also the prejudices which one has put ineradicably into one's head.

65. So much about noticing, where we find incompleteness and thus imperfection in psychognosy, but which (taken on its own) is still not a source for error, since there is no false noticing.

The same cannot be said of what we designated as the third task of the psychognost.

FIXING

1. We said that, to achieve his aim, the psychognost must achieve a multitude of things.

66

(a) He has to experience,
(b) he has to notice,
(c) he has to fix what he notices, in order to collect it,
(d) he has to generalize,
(e) he has to depriorize [*depriosieren*], recognize,[21f]
(f) he has to deduce.

Let us now turn to discuss the third point.

2. The particular which we notice is by itself of little importance.

To make use of what is noticed, we first have to put this insight [*Erkenntnis*] in relation to others, namely

(a) to other insights, future or past, of one's own; [and also]
(b) to insights of others, which will be both for their and one's own benefit.

3. In order to achieve this, it is necessary to take note of the particular noticed item [*das einzelne Bemerkte*], and to indicate it to others so that they can [also] take note of it. We indicate it to others by couching it in some language or other, and by communicating it to them so that they too will have permanent knowledge [*Kenntnis*] of it (maybe we had better disregard this for the moment). We [ourselves] will take note of it [i.e. the particular noticed item] by impressing it on our memory [*in unsere Erinnerung einprägen*], and 65|66 thus transforming it into a lasting insight. |

4. Nothing impresses itself explicitly on our memory which we have not noticed. But the fact that we do notice something is, by itself, not a sufficient condition for it to be added permanently to the treasure of our insights.

5. One will readily convince oneself of this if one considers that, for example, the distinction of visual intuition [*Gesichtsanschauung*] as a whole within the totality of our consciousness is already a noticing.

But clearly, in most cases, one will not retain the whole of a visual intuition in memory after a fleeting look, not even for a brief moment. Similar things can also occur thousandfold in simpler cases.

67

'Taking note [of something]' hence requires additional special conditions: the repetition of the impression.

It is useful for this purpose if we occupy ourselves vividly with an impression by which we are struck. This will tie this impression tightly to many other things, and thus occasion its revival [*Wiedererweckung*]. There is a lot being said about this in mnemonics, which, however, we shall not dwell on here.

There is just one factor which, due to its special importance, must be discussed in more detail. [It is the fact] that taking note of something is not always achieved by impressing that thing itself on our memory, but often by impressing on the memory something equivalent, something which stands in for [the thing we wish to take note of].

6. This sort of substitution [*Stellvertretung*] is, in many cases, advisable, indeed in some it is unavoidable, because it would often be difficult, if not impossible

(a) to revive the same presentational act *ad libitum*; or,
(b) if revived, to recognize it with certainty as being the same. [. . .]

7. But is this sort of substitution really possible?
How is one to conceive of it?
The simplest and most illustrative way of showing this is by means of examples.

8. We said that the psychognost has to fix what he notices in order to collect it. ¦

66¦67

And we have briefly pointed out the different means which he will have to use in order to achieve this.

In particular, [we talked] about [the fact] that, in some cases, he has to use a substitute presentation instead of a presentation which he himself might not be able to fix.

9. Such a substitute presentation is not [im]possible* because certain presentations stand in a peculiar relationship with other presentations. They are different from them, yet still point at them.

---

* The term in the German edition here is actually '*möglich*', i.e. 'possible', but since this does not seem to fit the context, I have chosen to interpret it as 'impossible' ('*unmöglich*').

They are, I would say, convertible with them; what falls under the one also belongs to the other. And they often correspond, if not perfectly, then at least to a considerable approximation, in their most important accomplishments [*Leistungen*].

Much of what associates with the one [presentation] also associates with the other.

If I look at the top of a round table from above, I judge the object thus appearing to me as being round, and the same happens if I look at it somewhat from the side. For I know that one and the same form [*Gestalt*], when looked at from different standpoints, creates different presentations. The presentations of an object which, under corresponding circumstances, creates one of these impressions are hence convertible with the presentations of an object which, under corresponding circumstances, creates the other one.

The situation is similar if I look at a vertical object with a vertical and a tilted head posture. I have very different presentations: in the second case, the object stimulates retinal areas which, had they been stimulated likewise with my head held vertically, would have led me to attribute a tilted position to the object. Yet, since I am conscious of tilting my head, I believe it to be in the same position as in the first case. The presentations of an object which under certain circumstances produces the one impression, and the presentations of an object which under corresponding circumstances produces the other impression, are convertible.

Both are thus tied to associations of the most varied kind.

67|68   Even the pleasure or displeasure tied to the phenomenon ¡ becomes, to some degree, something held in common [*etwas Gemeinsames*] (the lopsided impression [*schiefe Eindruck*] occurring in the case of a tilted head [*schiefe Kopfhaltung*] is not disturbing in the way it would be in the case of a vertical head posture).

We are in possession of an account by a famous composer (R. FRANZ)[21g] which, assuming he did not express himself in a totally inappropriate [or] wrong manner, would constitute a particularly curious case that would show to what extent presentations of completely different content may (sometimes) accomplish similar [things] with regard to [areas] where one would least likely expect it.

10. Unintuitive presentations [*unanschauliche Vorstellungen*] substitute for intuitive ones.

11. In other cases it happens that presentations substitute for presentations with a content that has a more superficial relationship to the content of the substituting ones.

(a) Convertibility. Correspondence between the essential accomplishments [in the context of] perspectival shifts (head posture, R. FRANZ).

(b) Unintuitive [things] substitute for negative intuitive [ones] and others.

(c) Causative [*kausative*] and affective relative determinations [substitute for] comparative relative determinations.

(d) We create such presentations with a clear intention when we define.

(e) In other cases, we create them without explicit (clear) consciousness of what happens within us.

(f) We create them for individual [things] as well as for general [ones].

(g) We have many of the same [kind].

(h) They are often much more composite than the ones they substitute for. And we are not clear about their content.

(i) We are neither clear about the relation between their contents [*inhaltliches Verhältnis*], nor about the one between their content and the content of the presentations they substitute for. [This is particularly true if we have a] tendency to identify them.

(k) This [leads to] erroneous opinions and psychognostic mistakes, in particular as far as the class of imaginary presentations of different concepts [*Phantasievorstellungen verschiedener Begriffe*] is concerned.

(l) It is well known that there are frequent shortcomings in the case of intentionally [*absichtlich*] given definitions.

(m) The same holds, of course, for the [sort of] substitute presentations which were created without explicit consciousness.

68|69 (n) Due to this, many different further aberrations [arise]. ¦

(o) A particular danger [exists] in the context of genetic determinations, due to the inexactness of the genetic laws [i.e. the laws of genetic psychology].

(p) In the context of comparative determinations, there is a particular danger
   (1) [to regard] as non-existing [*nicht vorhanden*] what is not noticed. MILL's correct remark: [that] saying 'Here is a rose'

70

is more than an expression of a perception; that this is also [an expression of] comparison.

(2) The ease of making an error in measuring ([say, if] the equal-noticeable [*Gleichmerkliches*]* [is taken to be] equal. – FECHNER's psycho-physical measurements [*Massbestimmungen*]).[22]

[We can, and indeed must take into account] things as heterogeneous as space and time, distances of length, tone and colour, as well as

habitual influences, influences of fatigue,

indeed, quite generally, degrees of attention, as [mentioned] above.

Alliance of differences (spatially, intensively and qualitatively different phenomena),

[to see] an inch as the increase to one inch and to one hundred inches; similar cases possibly in other contexts.[23]

(q) Habitual urge without clear consciousness of the basis [*Anhaltspunkte*] and of the probability of unification.

(r) Words and written language are substitute presentations of particular importance.

Recording [*Aufzeichnung*] is the most secure means of mediation for the future (although it always involves a certain [amount of] memory). Language is furthermore the means of intercourse with others.

(s) [It is thus] necessary for psychognosy to make linguistic determinations.

12. This shows how multifarious the dangers of imperfection and error are! In particular, one must be careful of

(a) rash denying due to not noticing;
(b) wrong measurements;
(c) confusion of what substitutes with what is substituted for, and *vice versa*.

---

* Brentano's use of the term '*gleichmerklich*', like Fechner's use of '*eben-merklich*' (see Note 22) is that of qualifying certain differences. There is thus the possibility (as suggested in the said note) that the two terms are actually synonymous. Yet, the way in which Brentano himself emphasizes that there is 'a connection *of some sort*' [p. 90, my emphasis] between the two concepts suggests that, at least for Brentano, such a synonymy was not self-evident. In order not to prejudge this issue, let me thus translate Brentano's '*gleichmerklich*' as 'equal-noticeable' and Fechner's '*eben-merklich*' as 'just-noticeable'.

([This is an error] similar to the one of equivocation and that
69|70   of confusing ¦ things strongly associated with what, in some
cases, may indeed only be associated in a very mediated manner.
ARISTOTLE's sphere, visually judging depths);

(d) a rash urge to name from memory [*gedächtnismässig*], i.e. habitually [*gewohnheitsmässig*], without investigating the particular
conditions for this urge; for example, [to call something] white
because [it is] brightest;

(e) the disadvantageous consequences which may result from the
imperfections of language:
1 equivocation,
2 vagueness of the concept,
3 unsuitability of the concept for substitution by not being
genuinely convertible.

[There is] no perfect language, indeed, no perfect science
(BENTHAM, COMTE) without a perfect psychognosy. (Consider the
difference between Roman and Arab numerals in the written language of arithmetic. Possible advantages of the dodecadic system.)

13. Instead of [carrying out] proper measurements (in the context of
a continuous manifold), it seems to be necessary to limit [oneself]
to counting equal-noticeable differences of fixed points, or, to
determine the point in its relation to a general and constant inclination [*Neigung*], for example, middle grey. [Is there] immediate
evidence [in the perception of middle grey]? Certainly not, but *de
facto* there is almost constancy. Generality – where might it derive
from? [There is] a connection of some sort with 'just-noticeability'
'*Eben-merklichkeit*'].

(Therefore, the concurrence [*Zusammenstimmen*]*, [but, I must
emphasize] the inadmissability of using this to construct an argument
for the equality of the equal-noticeable, contrary to what some
[people] might have thought.)

The present moment is also a fixed point [, namely] for time.

[There are] also fixed points of [the] region of clearest vision. (It
may be a blessing that not all of the retina is the same in this respect.
The horizontal [line] and – in an approximation – the vertical one
are fixed lines of the retina. [They go] through the region of clearest

* The verb '*zusammenstimmen*' is taken to be the same as '*übereinstimmen*', and, as
such, translated as 'to concur'.

70:71   vision; the relevant movements of ¦ the eye can be carried out with particular ease due to the muscular set-up.)

Fixed points [are determined] through psycho-physical genesis [*Genese*], for example [through] measurements with a pair of compasses, [through counting] the number of oscillations, [by using a] thermometer (on average), etc. [This involves an] imperfection, given by the fact that these are not the kind of measurements on which the most basic [*einfachsten*] genetical laws are grounded. This deficient state [of psychognostic studies] is lacking in purely psychological character [;something which], strictly speaking, goes against the spirit of psychognosy.

It also cannot be excluded that, on the basis of many experiences, the true numerical relations [*Massverhältnisse*] reveal themselves according to the principle of the higher probability of the simpler hypothesis.

14. So much about the third [task] which, as mentioned before, the psychognost must carry out, [namely] to fix what he notices in order to collect it.

INDUCTIVE GENERALIZATION

1. The fourth [task] which we identified [was] that he must generalize inductively.

2. It is not necessary for us to dwell on this point in the present context. Whatever is true in the other inductive sciences also applies here.

3. Obviously, due care is advised before one makes a claim that something generally does not exist [just] because we have not been able to notice it in experience.

(a) It has already been said that an individual [person] can be defective in his experiences. [But we have] also [mentioned] that this does not entail an incurable uncertainty.
(b) Likewise [it was stated] that our noticing can be defective; indeed, that this is so for almost all people.

However, by getting to know the conditions of noticing, we need not fear that this sort of uncertainty is given everywhere and incurably.

In many cases, we will be justified in making a claim with certainty: (for example, that there is no third quality apart from affirmation and negation. That there is no [pure] colour except red, yellow, blue, ¦ for instance, green, white, black and their mixtures).

71¦72

But due care [is] advised.

And if there is any chance left that there might be things which we or others have not noticed, then the more correct thing to say is: 'as far as one is, or has been able to notice', nothing else exists.

4. In the case of the peculiarities noticeable in certain elements of inner life, one must try to generalize as much as possible, so that the induction becomes exhaustive. That is to say, one must find the highest general concept involved in it [i.e. the induction] as peculiarity of species or genus [*Art- oder Gattungseigentümlichkeit*].

Otherwise it would be as if a mathematician, instead of introducing the theorem of the sum of the angles of triangles, were to introduce three theorems, namely one for polygons with right angles [*Rechtecke*], one for those with acute angles [*Spitzecke*] and one for those with obtuse angles [*Stumpfecke*].

For example,

[(a)] if an actually separable part of the experiential inner life [can be recognized, one must generalize in its terms]; or

[(b)] if, in experiencing a red [phenomenon] localized in a certain phenomenal point, one recognizes quality and spatial determination as mutually pervading parts of the content; and if one finds something similar in experiencing a blue [phenomenon] etc., in short, if one generally finds something similar in the domain of the visual sense, then we have to establish the connection between this characteristic with the actually separable colour-element in general [*das wirklich trennbare Farbenelement überhaupt*].

Similar things might be true in the case of sound, smell, taste and warmth, etc. Now, if it were indeed the case for the sensory element in general [*das Sinneselement überhaupt*], then this must be voiced.

5. But, be careful! [It is questionable] whether [in the context of sounds, smells, etc.,] spatial determination [*Örtlichkeit*], [or] quality can be used in the same sense [as above] or whether [they can] only

74

[be used] in analogy, in the way in which brightness or saturation [are] really only analogously [applicable to sounds, smells, etc.] supposing we wanted to say that a noise is an unsaturated sound in contrast to a sound that is a tone of the scale [–] if colour and tone [are only applicable by analogy].

6. In the latter case [i.e. quality and spatial determination being applicable to sounds, smells, etc. only by analogy], we clearly must regard the fact of there being an analogy as a general trait, and it is important to emphasize this. Similarly, we have to look in general for analogies as well as generalities. [Let me point out the] enormous importance of the ! knowledge of analogies in the different fields. (Not 72:73 identifying them is a psychognostic incompleteness which is usually connected with other [instances of] incompleteness).

By knowing the analogies everything becomes transparent, easier to grasp and to retain. (They [i.e. analogies] render a not unimportant service by simplifying the overall intuition [*Gesamtanschauung*] in giving it a more uniform character.)

[The knowledge of analogies] is also important for genetic psychology. *Nota bene*: In this context it is even valuable just to [work with] hypotheses on the basis of which [certain] things appear to be analogous which otherwise would not, as long as they [these hypotheses (a)] are in harmony with the known psychognostic and psychogenetic laws, [and (b)] possess genuine probability.

In a domain as interesting as this one, even insights which are merely probable [*Wahrscheinlichkeitserkenntnis*] and which have only little, if any, chance of ever becoming certain [knowledge], are of value.

7. The psychognost must intuitively grasp the general laws wherever the necessity or impossibility of unifying certain elements becomes clear through the concepts themselves. There are many cases like this, partially concerning purely distinctional elements [and] partially [concerning] separable ones.

For example, the peculiarity of evidence is not to be found anywhere outside of judgments. And, as little as it is to be found outside the domain of judgment, as little will it be possessed by each and every kind of judgment. There are affirmative judgments with a matter [*Materie*] containing a possibly hidden conflict of determinations. They are never evident. There is absolute incompatibility.

In contrast, we must admit a curious case of necessary connection, for example, in the case of the determination of place. Each [and every] point in a phenomenal space is of a specific spatial species. Each one is different in spatial species from every other one, no matter how little they are distanced [from one another]. A point [in a phenomenal space] may possibly even continue to exist if some other point which previously coexisted with it is no longer phenomenally given, and [indeed] even if there is no [phenomenally given] point which has the same spatial species as the [previously coexisting] one. ¦

73¦74

But [a phenomenal point] cannot exist on its own. It can only exist in the context of innumerably many others which are [phenomenally] given at the same time, and which form a multidimensional continuum with it. It might possibly be an endpoint, but certainly not an endpoint in every direction. It has the characteristics of a border, which [itself] never is, nor could be, something on its own.

[I refer to the] absurdities in SUAREZ's[23a] [work].[24] Thus a certain case of inseparability [is acknowledged]. Similar things are true of the temporal species. There are thus actual cases where the necessity or impossibility of certain connections of elements of inner life become immediately clear from the concepts [themselves]. And nothing of this is refuted by the fact that, here [i.e. in the context of spatial and temporal continua] as elsewhere, the verity of [there being] a priori evidence has been denied, indeed [nothing is refuted by the fact] that worthy scientists have put forward theories which in their very foundations made assumptions contradicting these axioms.

For example, [the] punctualists, [or] FECHNER's[24a] theory of philosophical atomism.[25] Naturally, we must again be careful, for at least as often, if not more so, it has happened that, in being misled by the the urge of habit or whatever else, someone incorrectly declared something to be an immediate axiom.

So much, in short, concerning the fifth point.

MAKING DEDUCTIVE USE

1. 'He [the psychognost] has to make deductive use of what he gained in one way or another (inductively or intuitively) from the general laws.'

76

We claimed that by doing this he will be able to find an answer to many a question concerning the elements which otherwise he would barely have been able to answer.

A simple example arises in the context of what we have just said about the character of the spatial determination.

We can conclude from this that the contents of sensory experiences [*Inhalte der Sinnesempfindungen*] are in truth continua, (even though at any ¦ [particular] identifiable point it is not certain whether there is not actually a gap which is simply too small to be noticed).

74¦75

[This constitutes,] thus, a certain substitute for the shortcomings of noticing, although it is not a perfect one.

Another example can be found by looking back at the previously mentioned case of the individuality of the content of inner perception.

It is clear from the beginning that in the same way as there are no species without differences, there is no individual without an individualizing difference.

An individually occurring phenomenon, [or] an individual content must contain an individualizing factor. But we are incapable of noticing it. Its existence is thus established purely deductively. In using certain inductively obtained insights which provide us with clues for explaining this most striking phenomenon, we are able to add further conclusions. For example, [we can conclude that] the individualizing element is constant, [that] it is exactly the same [*unterschiedslos*] in all the phenomena which are stored in memory [and] according to which we have fresh experiences [*frisch erleben*].[26]

Let me be brief at this point. The elaborations which are to follow will richly illustrate this sixth point, as well as the preceding ones.

2. This concludes the list of what the psychognost has to perform in order to achieve his aims.

I believe that [in establishing it] we have gained a deeper insight into the peculiar difficulties of psychognostic research than was given to us merely by the fact of [there being] greatly varying and contradicting opinions [*grosse und mannigfache Gegensätze der Meinungen*].

We have identified the general sources of imperfections and errors.

We have also characterized, at least to some degree, the method by means of which we can successfully and with certainty avoid these errors and find the truth.

Accordingly, we are approaching our task with much essential help and encouragement. Yet, admittedly, [we are approaching it] also with the realization that our task is a difficult one, which demands patience, practice, prudence, [or,] in brief, the most taxing

75|76   attentiveness. ǀ

But, in view of the special value of the insights we are here struggling to attain, this should not be a deterrent.

PSYCHOGNOSY AS PRECONDITION FOR GENETIC PSYCHOLOGY

1. This is why psychognosy is so extraordinarily valuable. Indeed, if we dwell briefly on the value of our discipline, I have no doubt that we must admit that the main value of psychognosy is given in its providing a basis for genetic psychology. What is dependent on it? Logic, ethics, aesthetics, economics, politics, sociology.

2. But, [this is] not [to say that] it [i.e. psychognosy] is not very valuable by itself.

(a) Theoretical [value]:
   (1) It acquaints us with the objects [*Gebilde*]* of our own self,
   (2) and with this with the highest and most noble that exists in the realm of experience.
   (3) The things it is concerned with are intuitive to us in the way they really are.
      In this respect, [psychognosy] differs essentially from the whole of natural science.
      Explanation:.
      AMPÈRE: 'How should I avoid the land full of flowers and living waters, how leave rivers and pastures for deserts scorched by that mathematical sun which only throws the brightest light on things, in order to wilt them and to dry them out down to the roots . . .'
      Nota bene: The whole of natural science, almost like mathematics, is of interest for psychical matters essentially only as an instrument, [or] as an influencing factor.
      [The same is true for] medicine – indeed even for geology

---

*   '*Gebilde*' can mean 'object', but also 'creation' or 'pattern'.

78

and astronomy [– because of the] darkness of the subject matter in question in itself.

76ː77 (b) The practical value is given by its *characteristica universalis* ¦ (LEIBNIZ).

[This finds its expression also in the letter of] DESCARTES to Père
77ː78 MERSENNE.# ¦

\# 'If someone were to explain correctly what are the simple ideas in the human imagination out of which all human thoughts are compounded, and if his explanation were generally received, I would dare to hope for a universal language very easy to learn, to speak and to write. The greatest advantage of such a language would be the assistance it would give to men's judgement, representing matters so clearly that it would be almost impossible to go wrong. [. . .]

I think it is possible to invent such a language and to discover the science on which it depends: it would make peasants better judges of the truth about the world than philosophers are now. But do not hope ever to see such a language in use. For that, the order of nature would have to change so that the world turned into a terrestrial paradise; and that is too much to suggest outside of fairyland.' [Descartes to Mersenne, 20 November 1629; *Oeuvres de Descartes*, AT I, 81; tr. by A. Kenny in *Descartes: Philosophical Letters*; Oxford 1970, p. 6.]

Part II

A SURVEY OF PSYCHOGNOSY

1

THE COMPONENTS OF HUMAN CONSCIOUSNESS

79   1. We said psychognosts are searching for the components of human consciousness; they attempt to determine, if possible exhaustively, its elements and the ways in which they are connected.

2. This presupposes that consciousness is not something simple. And this is undeniable.

The objection based on the unity of consciousness which some [people] might put forward is invalid. It is not as if the unity of consciousness could reasonably be denied: but, as stated already by ARISTOTLE, unity is not the same as simplicity.

3. We have seen how parts in human consciousness can be distinguished in two ways:

(a) In one case we are dealing with things where the one can actually be separated from the other.
(b) The other case deals with things where the one can be distinguished from the other.

   (Actually separable [parts] – merely distinctional parts.)

4. The actually separable [parts] were, in part mutually, in part one-sidedly separable. We also found that often they themselves again contain parts which are actually separable. If this ceases to be the case for certain parts, then we can call these, in the sense of actual separability indivisible, parts 'elements' of human consciousness.

5. The merely distinctional parts were also multifarious. We distinguished above all two classes.

(a) Distinctional parts in the strict sense, [and]
(b) parts gained through modifying distinction.

In the first class we have

(1) mutually pervading (concrescent[26a]) parts,
79¦80　(2) logical parts, ¦
(3) the merely distinctional parts of the psychical di-energy,
(4) the parts of the intentional pair of correlates.

As parts which are to be gained through modifying distinction we mentioned:

(1) the objects in the act and in its intentional correlate, [and]
(2) the parts of these parts (that is of the objects) in manifold ways.

6. Similar to the case of actually separable parts there are some amongst the merely distinctional [parts] which, in contrast to others, do not contain any further parts. They are hence ultimate purely distinctional elements.

7. We have seen that the psychognost who wants to investigate the elements in the sense of ultimate actually separable parts will not get around the question concerning the elements in the sense of ultimate distinctional parts.

(a) Otherwise, no clear description would be possible; [and]
(b) an unmentionable multiplication of determinations would result. In the case [of vision] alone, [there would be] as many names, if not more, as there are points in the visual field.
(c) The differentiation of a purely distinctional part makes up the essence of parts which are particularly separable [*besonders abtrennbar*].

8. These are the points which I had to recall before I was able to continue the investigation.

9. The next question concerns the order of explanation in the synopsis which is now to begin.

10. I could start with an index of the merely distinctional parts and

then turn to the exposition of the actually separable elements by making use of the merely distinctional parts in describing them.

11. However, I do not believe that this order is to be recommended. Even though we do not insist on proving everything put forward in the synopsis, I would nonetheless not wish to structure the explanation in a way in which everything would be given without foundation. And this would, at least initially, be the case for the register of merely distinctional parts.

80:81 It would not in any way be intuitive [to the reader] that this register of distinctional elements really is ¦ accurate and exhaustive (apart from certain shortcomings arising from the difficulty of the question and the incompleteness of present-day research) for human consciousness.

In order to avoid this, we must, one by one, go through the cases [*Gebiete*] where the merely distinctional parts can be found. And these cases will surely be actually separable parts.

12. Actual separability, we said, is often one-sided. In this case one part is more independent of the other than *vice versa*. It appears to be natural to start with the most independent parts.

13. Yet, we will not start with a description of the most independent case. Indeed, we will totally refrain from giving such a description, with the possible exception of some negative and relative specifications.

14. The astonishment which this remark may cause will presumably abate immediately when I say that the most independent of the actually separable parts of human consciousness is the one individuating it.

15. Previous elaborations have already led us to mention this fact. Let us re-examine briefly what has been said; for the matter is of importance; implications of the highest importance even for metaphysics are tied to it. Even in itself, it is of the highest interest. [This is why I add the following] brief discussion.

16. I said that we can give some negative and relative determinations of it [i.e. the most independent of the actually separable parts of

human consciousness].* So, for example, that it is not spatial, [and] that it does not change [anywhere] within the realm of our thought.

Proof: Because of inner perception, the space which it [i.e. IP] would show us would have to be actually taken up by it. But then [there would] surely soon [be] another rapid change of location with the body. And then [there would be] considerable, [and thus] securely noticeable [*mit sicherer Merklichkeit*], differences.

[The IP] consequently [does] not [have] length, breadth, depth, [nor is it] round or square and so forth. With equal certainty [it can be concluded that it is] without colour and other sensory qualities (and without mass).

81¦82

Objection: What if [the space which the IP would show us were] unnoticeably small?

Answer: If [the space] were unnoticeably small, then whatever fills it would also be unnoticeable, [and] hence the whole [would be] psychical.

17. In relative terms we can describe it [the IP] by saying that it individuates, and is implicitly given in every human act of consciousness.

18. It continues to exist in all probability when we are asleep or unconscious. Whether [it does so] purely on its own or together with other psychical parts like sensations etc. can probably not be decided with certainty. The fact [is] that when we wake up, we often do not remember any dream. – There are some people who declare that in their whole life they have not had a dream, and are reluctant to believe what you tell them about the subject matter.

Yet [it is] certain that sometimes, even though we do not remember any dream, we nonetheless have had one and we produce clear signs of it.

DESCARTES and LEIBNIZ thus have not hesitated to claim resolutely that something like sensation [or a] dream is always present.

Are they justified in this?

It seems that if we tire, there is some kind of decrease of psychical acts. Why [should it] thus [be] impossible that at least

* In order to facilitate explanatory cross-referencing, I shall use 'IP' (for 'individuating part') to refer to this most independent of the actually separable parts of human consciousness.

from time to time all that remains is that constant individualizing component which in itself we cannot determine positively?

19. However, a psychognost does not, as such, have to investigate the question which [of these options] is the more correct or more probable one.

20. [Is the IP] without intentional relation to itself? It [the IP] may seem to affirm it [the intentional relation]! For otherwise it would not be contained [*mitbeschlossen*] in our consciousness ([as] a pervading part with two others). [It is] not improbable (if not certain) that, like other things, [the IP] works intentionally. There would otherwise be no di-energy.

82¦83
21. However, regarding such an obscure element, the psychognost must content himself [with little]. His task is achieved if he manages to demonstrate the actual presence of the mysterious element. ¦

22. So much about the fundamental reality from which everything which otherwise belongs to the inner life of a person is separable, and by which everything belonging to our self is individualized.

23. Let us [now] look at the other parts which are to be distinguished with regard to actual separability, [parts] which we shall call psychical acts.

2

PSYCHICAL ACTS

INTRODUCTION

As regards psychical acts, we wish to identify, above all,

(a) what they have in common, [and]
(b) the main classes they fall into.

[I can be] brief as far as the first question is concerned, for most, if not all [of the relevant points have] already [been] discussed:

(1) They [psychical acts] involve the individualizing reality [i.e. IP] (similar to [the way in which] logical differences [involve] the genus).
(2) Like it, they are without location, spatial extension, etc.
(3) Like it, they are without colour etc.
(4) They have [an] intentional relation [*intentionale Beziehung*].
(5) They have di-energy, primary–secondary relation.
(6) The secondary relation is a presenting and a judging, [or] believing, which [is] simply assertoric, yet evident.

The general claim has been made that a feeling of pleasure or displeasure [is] also [assertorically evident]; but this without any rigorous proof or maybe even without any plausibility.

Indeed, as certainly (obviously) as it [i.e. assertoric evidence] does occur sometimes, as certainly (probably) ought it to be missing in other cases. ([Otherwise] one would have to say [that we are dealing with an] unnoticeably small intensity.)

One should also not believe that evident perception always carries the character of apperception (of noticing: connected with LEIBNIZ' *apercevoir*). |

TWO MAIN CLASSES: FUNDAMENTAL ACTS
AND SUPERPOSED ACTS

1. With regard to the second question concerning the classes into which psychical acts can be divided, two main classes are, above all, to be distinguished [,namely]

(a) [the one of] fundamental [acts, and]
(b) [the one of] superposed [*supraponiert*] acts.

Superposed acts are related to fundamental ones similar to the way in which the fundamental ones are related to the psychical substratum. Examples:

(1) [The] presenting of the general concept of colour, or of blueness, or of lightness.
    (The basis of this is the intuition of a concrete colour phenomenon at such and such a location, of such and such a size, outlined by this or that shape.)

(2) [The] wish to go on a journey.
    (This is based on the presentation of the journey.)

(3) [The] belief that no [number] two is dissimilar to another one.
    (Basis: The presentation of a two, [a presentation] which is unequal to some other one.)

(4) [The] unintuitive presentation of a black grey [*Schimmel*].
    (Sensory intuition of a black [thing], a grey [thing] and intuitions of other components, the detailed specification of which is to be reserved for a later investigation.)

2. Amongst the superposed acts are many which, relative to others, may again be called fundamental. For example, conjecture [relative] to fear or hope, the belief in the impossibility in the case of dispair.

Nota bene: Fear [is] not a uniform genus, but a uniform, separable part (or a part separable from it).

In a first instance, we collect all of them in the second main class of superposed psychical act.

90

THE NATURE OF FUNDAMENTAL
PSYCHICAL ACTS

1. If we look at those psychical acts which, in being fundamental,
84:85 belong to the first main class, [we will see that] they are without
exception acts which have sensory phenomena as primary objects.
That is to say, they contain as primary relation a presenting of
concrete sensory content.

Example: Every sensory experience, be it a so-called objective
one, or a subjective one like a hallucination, or some middle thing
like certain illusions.

Amongst the objective [sensory experiences] are reflex experiences as well as the ones which are excited without mediation
[*unmittelbar erregt*], [say, through the excitation] of an internally or
externally located nerve ending.

And like the [sensory experiences arising] from a peripheral
excitation of nerve endings, the ones arising from an excitation at a
non-peripheral point of a nerve strand are also objective (the little
mouse in the case of the *nervus ulnaris* of an amputated person).

Again, one should count all, or at least most of the so-called after-
images to this group.

It has been shown how negative after-images are excited from the
peripheral end-organ or, at least, from a station which lies on the way
to the central terminus (provided, [according to EBBINGHAUS,[26b]] that
no earlier positive after-image supersedes the stronger negative one).
There is certainly also a part of the positive after-images which is
excited from a point not less distanced from the central terminus than
the negative one.

The other ones may [be excited] from an intermediate station.

Another example [of a fundamental psychical act] is [given in]
every proteraesthesis,* that is, every *proterosis* belonging to a
sensory experience.[26c] [It occurs, for example, in the] visual intuition
of rest or motion or discolouring, [in the] so-called hearing of a word,
a syllable, a sequence of sounds which are sung or which are created
by a musical instrument.

The great similarity and the close genetic tie with the experiences
concerned was the reason that it [proteraesthesis] was for a long time
generally confounded with sensations. The components belonging to
proteraesthesis are even today often counted as components of sensations.

---

* *Proter* (Greek for 'earlier') + *aesthesis* (Greek for 'perception').

85|86   LOCKE, LEIBNIZ and many physiologists and ¦ psychologists of today still speak, like ARISTOTLE, of experiences of motion.

2. Indeed, we will show that a sensation is nothing on its own, that it only exists as boundary of a proterosis – however not as a boundary in the sense of a *terminus intra* but in the sense of a *terminus extra*.

3. As concerns their [i.e. the fundamental psychical acts'] general characteristics, [we will have to consider] the following [kinds of] remarks.

(a) Those pertaining to the relation to the primary object, [and]
(b) those [pertaining] to the relation to the secondary one.

4. The relation to the primary object seems to be without exception a dual one:

(1) a presenting, [and]
(2) a blind assertoric accepting.

5. The last [point] could raise some reservations. For it to be correct, it is not sufficient if this [blind assertoric accepting occurs concomitantly just] sometimes: it must [occur] always and prove to be inseparable [from the sensation]. ARISTOTLE seems to be in favour of it. In the two-finger experiment[27] one of the senses maintains the claim even though the other one contradicts it. Against this there is, however, a very tempting argument: the conviction which the scientifically educated [people] nowadays customarily have [, namely] that colours, sounds etc. do not exist in reality. Indeed, even the less enlightened [ones] really no longer succumb to every perceptual deception of mirroring, of light refraction in water, etc. Having become more clever through experience, they now judge the outside world concerning sensory impression differently than they did earlier; they reject as false what earlier they most likely would have taken to be true. One could only maintain that they still take it to be true if one meant by this that they simultaneously take it to be true and false, which obviously would be a considerable paradox!

Now, if this argument is found to be convincing, then the belief in the sensory phenomenon, where it exists, will not belong inseparably to the fundamental psychical act. It is rather to be seen as a particular superposed act.

6. Yet the argument is not as conclusive as it might seem at this
86¦87 stage. ¦

(a) The contrast between accepting and rejecting is not stronger than
the one between loving and hating. If it is thus possible to
simultaneously love and hate the same thing, then it does not
seem to be excluded from the outset that one simultaneously
accepts and rejects the same thing.

Yet the [hypothetical point] concerning the conflict between
affect and higher emotion seems to be correct.

(b) Many (for example, HELMHOLTZ) speak of the continuation of
optical illusions, even after the error has been recognized. (The
instinctive urge to believe may be founded in, or given by habit).

In rational people the recognition [of the error] will, of course,
predominate. They will guide their actions according to it. Yet it
can also happen that, in the case of a momentary reduced
attentiveness, it [the recognition of error] is again superseded
[verdrängt] by the instinctive error, similar to the way in which,
so to speak, higher emotional activity is overcome and swept
away by affects.

(c) [This can be compared to] the way in which general concepts are
denied, even though they are thought explicitly and thus noticed
evidently, yet judged incorrectly.

Particular evidence in favour of the belief in the primary object
being contained in the fundamental act is provided by reflections
arising from the question concerning the origin of the belief in
an external world.

These reflections seem to lead to [the conclusion] that rather
than having originally been without such a belief, [and] having
only gained it later by realizing that the law-governed connection
between the sequence of our psychical experiences can be best
understood on the basis of such hypotheses, one did trust
immediately, as in [the case of] memory.

The belief [contained] in the fundamental sensory acts thus
seems to be involved in the beginning. And since they [the
fundamental acts] themselves remain in nature unchanged, no
matter how much our inner life develops and enriches itself over
and above them, we may conclude for each one of us that this
first primitive belief is never exterminated. Rather it is merely
87¦88 overcome, ¦ and in a certain sense suppressed, held down [and]
deprived of its old influence [in ihrem Einflusse kontrariert] by

93

higher acts of judgment which are motivated as being insights gained through reasoning or something similar.

(d) One should not be misled by [the fact] that it is possible to think that one does not have the belief [in question], for

(1) the belief is often not explicit; [and]

(2) the bogus argument mentioned above may lead to the claim [that there is no such belief], in the manner in which bogus arguments lead to the denial of general concepts, even though the denier thinks them explicitly and may use them like other [concepts] in general judgments [or] conclusions.

This is why even today ARISTOTLE's old view recommends itself as being probably the correct one.

Yet I would not wish to say that it has been established with certainty by the above discussion. For there is yet another view which in one way or another remains conceivable: namely, that the instinctive belief in the primary object was originally tied to sensation, yet only as a second, superposed act, which, at the time, sprang causally from it; later, however, this belief no longer comes into effect because of other inhibiting factors.

7. Only experience can decide. I have already expressed my view that ARISTOTLE's conception seems to be correct. The facts concur. And [he] also recommends the most simple of intuitions.

THE PRIMARY OBJECTS OF FUNDAMENTAL [PSYCHICAL] ACTS

Two Mutually Pervading Parts: Spatial Determination [*Räumlichkeit*] and Quality

1. The primary objects of fundamental acts (that is of experiences 88!89 and proteraestheses) share a number of striking properties which ¦ distinguish them from those of other psychical acts. I mentioned that they are concreta of mutually pervading parts.

These concreta display, without exception, the following components, whose nature and mutual relation, will, in many cases, reveal itself best by considering the particular.

[The reason for this is that] the layman has a very confused view of many of them, and often we can only achieve a clearer insight by summoning all the auxiliary means of induction, intuition [*Intuition*] and deduction.

2. At first I shall just list them one by one. All primary objects of fundamental acts

(a) have a specific spatial or space-like [*raumähnliche*] determination. (One of their pervading [parts] is spatial determination or [its] analogue.)

(b) They have a second specific determination which, as a pervading part of the spatial determination, occupies the place (or, the analogue of the place), [i.e.] fills the space (or the analogue). In the case of experiences (and presumably also in the one of proterosis) these second specific determinations are called qualities (colour in the widest sense, tone or its analogue).

The Components of Quality

1. Within that which is called quality (or analogue of quality) in the wider sense, we can distinguish two more components,

(a) lightness or darkness (or [the] analogue [thereof]),
(b) saturation or unsaturatedness (or [the] analogue [thereof]).

Instead of saturation, one could also say colouredness [*Kolorit*], or sonance [*Sonanz*], by generalizing expressions which at first were used in a more narrow experiential field.

[This is so] because in the domain of visual experience, the contrast between saturation and unsaturatedness occurs as that between colouredness [*Farbigkeit*] in the narrow sense and colourlessness of visual phenomena – black, white, grey.

And similarly, in the domain of auditory experience, it occurs as the [contrast] between the sonorous, or tonal [*klanghaft*] and the toneless [*klanglos, tonlos*] – bangs and other noises.

We shall see that analogous [contrasts] occur in all sensory domains.[28]

89;90

2. As concerns these two components (lightness and saturation) the question arises: are they two different, mutually pervading parts like place and quality? Or, are some [of them], like, for example, the (un-)saturated [ones], species of the same genus which are simply distinguished in a particular way? [. . .]

(a) like, e.g., if someone were to think that the saturated [components] alone give rise to affects, or that they give rise to other affects than the unsaturated [ones],

95

(b) or, if someone else were to say: the determinations and differences of lightness, colouredness [*Koloritheit*] and unsaturatedness [*Sättigungslosigkeit*] relate to one another like the
determinations [and differences, respectively] of the position of
a point according to height, width and depth; ([i.e. according to
a] multitude [*Mehrheit*] of coordinates, while space, after all, is
of one genus).

(One could, e.g., compare colour lightness with height, [and]
the difference of colouredness or unsaturatedness at equal lightness with temporal distances.)

The completely unsaturated [phenomena] would then have the
distinction of, so to speak, belonging to the straight line of the
lightest and darkest colour quality.

3. At this stage, we do not yet wish to settle the question, since we
are already able to recognize independently that, at present, we are
in any case not justified by the double contrast of lightness and
darkness, saturation and unsaturatedness to say that we have found
more than two general components.

For if colouredness [*Farbenhaftigkeit*] were a particular genus,
then colourlessness would not be a positive but a privative contrast
[to colouredness]; like evidence to blindness in the case of judgments. Yet we are at this stage only dealing with the general
characteristic. Thus we are, for the moment, left with just place and
quality.

But then two more [components] seem to be added, namely
intensity and purity or mixture [*Gemischtheit*] (quality, simplicity or
multiplicity, or analogues [thereof]).

4. There are, however, many [different] views about the nature of
the one and the other. Concerning the purity or mixture discerned in
90¦91   colours, [some] important ¦ scientists claim, for instance, that colours
are actually all of equal simplicity, yet some are, so to speak, corner
colours, the others edge, surface and interior intermediate colours
[see Figure 1].

5. Again, in the case of tones, it is claimed that we are given the
faculty of a two-, three- and even higher fold sensory field with the
same spatial species. Or, rather [it is claimed] there is not a conflict
in filling a place, but rather penetrability. Space [it is said] is filled
two, indeed n-times, and one filling is said to exist as if the other did

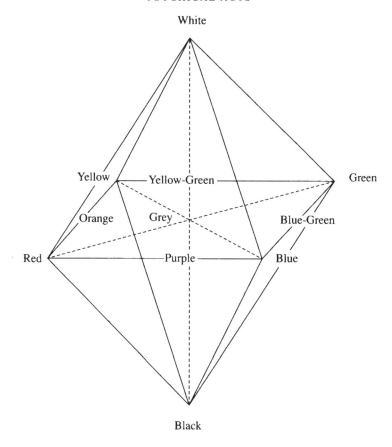

Figure 1
Source: Boring 1933[29]

not. (Such that there would be different qualities of mutually pervading parts like place and quality.)

6. According to this, the multiplicity in the case of vision would be completely different from the one of hearing, yet in neither case would it be a particular pervading part [*besonders durchwohnender Teil*].

7. These views are probably untenable. I do believe though, that we shall clearly see that in the correct view, the difference of simplicity

97

91|92 or multiplicity will also not require us to assume a third pervading part. ¦ And likewise, it might turn out that it is only due to confused presenting that we are tempted to see intensity[30] as a particular pervading part of the primary object. This temptation is, at any rate, something which is to be found in a characteristic analogous way in all known domains of fundamental acts. (Short explanation concerning unnoticeably small parts.)

Is Temporal Determination [*Zeitlichkeit*] a Third Part?

1. So, up to now we still only have two mutually pervading parts which are generally contained in the primary object of every fundamental act: place and quality (or, the analogue [thereof]). And that seems to be the end of the matter, except that we might identify temporal determination [*Zeitbestimmung*] as a third one.

2. Indeed, it [temporal determination] can be found in proteraesthesis which displays a past time interval. If it can also be found in sensation, then we would truly have a new general particularity of all fundamental acts.

3. [Let us consider the following five arguments] in favour [of this].

(1) If [the] past is shown to us by proterosis, then it appears to sensation as [the] present. Yet [the] present seems to be as much a temporal species as any past points in time. Past, present, future.
(2) Sensation is continually connected [*in kontinualem Zusammenhang*] to proterosis because of the *terminus extra* (the closing boundary). It seems that, as such, it must belong to the genus.
(3) Take two cases of regular and continuous temporal variation, which are distinguished by the [fact that] one runs twice as fast as the other. We will find that the same quantity of temporal species is associated, on the one hand, with half, on the other, with double the quantity of the species of the second variable.

92|93 This is something which has often raised astonishment; indeed, in many cases it was regarded as a contradiction. (It was thought ¦ that we are dealing here with two unequal magnitudes which are both equal to a third one.) There is no contradiction, but we are here dealing with something which, when not carefully described, can very easily lead to an entanglement in contradictions. We will try to elucidate this question later when we shall

98

talk about the particularity of continua, amongst which an outstanding position is, apart from time, primarily taken up by space. Yet it will already at this stage be clear that where the same quantity [*Menge*] of species of one genus [say T] [(where] each [species] occurs only once[)] is coordinated now with a smaller, now a bigger quantity of species of a different genus [say C], the mode of coordination [*Zuordnungsmodus*] and that of continuity must be different. In the slower change the [C-]continuum appears to be temporally [i.e. with respect to T] more dilated, [whereas] in the swifter one, every [C-species] is brought temporally closer to every other one. They [the C-species] are, so to speak, more compressed. The fact that, in the one case, the whole quantity of [C-]species fills out double the amount [in T than in the other case] is reflected also in the cases of half, one-hundredth, etc. [of the quantity of C-species]. The mode of coordination which makes the whole fill out double as much time, shows the same [characteristic right] down to the infinitesimal. Each colour species [in this case] somehow manages [to fill out] the double [amount of time].

In the same way in which the mode of coordination remains unchanged regarding every point of the past, so also regarding the point of the present. That [is so] now, where the union is shown to us by sensation, as [does] proterosis in the case of past moments.

Even if it [sensation], as concerns the present, is showing us a different mode of coordination of the temporally varying component from what it is tied to (that is to say, the Now), then this [the Now] must [none the less] bear the general temporal character like any past moment. Sensation shows, if not differences of before and after, at least differences of being temporally situated, and this is sufficient to prove that a temporal determination constitutes a pervading part of sensation as it does in the case of proterosis.

(4) If two species with a finite difference from one another are realized in space as bordering one another, then the borders will coincide.
93|94 (It is in this sense that two, indeed several straight lines between two points are possible.) Something analogous is true of temporal boundaries. And obviously not just of temporal boundaries which are in the past or in the future, but also of [the temporal boundary which is] the present. At the moment of change, both [past and future] are actual and the sudden change falls into the present.

But where there is change, there is temporal determination.

Thus, temporal determination is given in sensation as in proterosis. Accordingly, [we find] this particular pervading part also [in sensation].

(5) A further, fifth reason could be put forward [in support of the claim] that sensation, which does not display any past, must nonetheless show the boundary of the past with a clearly homogeneous (temporal) character. Whatever inner perception[31] does show to us, like sensation, it does not show it as being past. But sometimes it seems to reveal to us clearly the connection with the past. I am thinking of the cases where it shows us an affecting [*Wirken*] and a being affected [*Gewirktwerden*]. [For example, in the cases of] premises, conclusion, motivation of desiring, etc.

This affecting and being affected is not the same as succession *per se* (or regular succession or necessary succession). Yet it seems to contain the presentation of temporal contiguity; only the temporally adjoining [*zeitlich Angrenzendes*] creates the temporally adjoining, [only] the earlier [creates] the later. Temporal contiguity and continuity seem to reveal themselves in what inner perception shows in this case. Hence, it clearly seems to possess temporal character.

But the same will surely be true of every other case of inner perception, and consequently presumably also of the (primary) object of sensation.

4. These arguments may be impressive. Yet there remains a doubt.

A past N is not an N. It is modified. A present N is an N, at least it does not have any modifying temporal determination. Does it have an enriching one? How does it differ from N itself? Is the true N not *eo ipso* a presently existing N? It does not seem to be possible here 94|95 to find anything similar as in the case of other enriching attributes. |

5. Maybe it is none the less possible to counter these arguments by simply acknowledging what undoubtedly must be acknowledged, [namely] that sensation (in particular the one which we are focusing on) never occurs separated from proterosis.

6. (a) The present is often taken in a wider [and] often in a narrower sense. In the most narrow sense it is only [a] point. It is seldom used in this way. But here it can only be considered in this most narrow sense. And in this case it could be some sort of zero point. Modifying determinations [would be] on both sides.

Here, in any case, [we do not have] any modifying ones. Why not? [Don't we have] any at all? Such that the object is real [here, and] not real there?

(b) These points should already be sufficient to show that this argument is based on dubious foundations. Consider further the increase of an intensity from a zero point, or any other continuous growth from zero. The same formula of variation can hold, and yet a point, as boundary, [can be a] zero [-point].

7. It was thus possible to counter these two arguments.
But what about the other three?
I must admit that I, for one, cannot see an escape route.

8. This leaves us no option but to see whether it might not be possible to counter the counter-argument.

This might be possible in the following manner. Let us admit that the outermost boundary point to which the past time stretches does, by itself, not contain any modifying and enriching determinations, such that one would really be dealing with a type of zero point. [In this case] it remains none the less true that this point does not exist by itself. It only exists as a boundary.

And it seems that the way in which it forms the boundary of what is bound [by it] cannot be completely indifferent in this context, as little as if it were a point in proterosis which does contain a determined modifying temporal species.

Clarification by means of a simile:

95¦96 (a) A body is thrown up vertically. We have a highest ¦ point. Temporally, this is a kind of zero point of rising and falling, yet it can hardly be called a point of rest, for up to it and beginning with it there is motion (a point which as boundary point separates two motions, a rising one and a falling one).

(b) The same body which was thrown up vertically, the same initial velocity but the mass of the earth being doubled.

We would again have a highest point to be reached. It [too] would be a kind of temporal zero point of rising and falling.

Yet [there is] a difference to the earlier case.

(1) [The body] does not [rise] as high.

(2) The decrease and increase in the speed of the motion [is] throughout a quicker one. The mode of continuity in the zero

101

point is thus essentially different [from the one in the initial example].

9. This appears to be the correct mediation between the pro and contra in this context.

10. Even if this [by itself] does not allow us to say that sensation and its primary object have nothing to do with temporal determination, this [statement] will immediately become true if we allow ourselves to consider sensation by itself, [i.e.] by fictitiously dissolving its connection with proterosis. In this case the temporal will be completely excluded.

Explanation by means of the above simile. In the isolated moment of the highest height the body would rest. There would remain no trace of the falling motion in it, and naturally all differences of the mode of falling, of the mode of succession, of individual stages of motion, etc. would simultaneously be disregarded.

([The situation is] similar in the case of a [uniform] circular motion [of two bodies with the same mass and the same angular speed] with double the radius and the same tangential force. The centripetal force [could be taken to] cease to act in the [relevant] places: [in which case the bodies would have to be seen as moving] rectilinearly with the same speed. [The difference] between the mode of curvature of the big and that of the small circle would have no influence.)[31a]

11. Thus, if we consider sensation and proteraesthesis separately we will have to speak of ¦ temporal determination as a pervading part only in the case of proteraethesis.

96¦97

12. Mind you, someone might say that this is not really a full justification. We made a mistake in treating sensation separately. We ourselves admitted that in reaching the conclusion we made use of a fiction, and this gives rise to the falsification.

However, it seems to me the fiction is of a completely innocent kind. As it is made in full consciousness it cannot lead to errors.

Do not mathematicians time and time again introduce similar fictions! For us it carries a big representational advantage in that it allows us to begin with the more simple [things]. We want to describe the elements of inner life. In the case of the continuous, what else could this be than the individual boundary? – If this is not admitted,

102

one would have to say that in this context there are no elements but only what in successive reduction approaches an element in the infinite.

13. The practical advantage, of which I am talking here, emerges even more forcefully [and] in its full significance if we take the following question into account:

Is the analogue of a concretum of quality and spatial determination [*Örtlichkeit*], which we called the primary object of sensory proterosis, exhaustively and with full accuracy described if one says it consists of past concreta of quality and spatial determination?

By careful scrutiny of the state of affairs one will find reasons for denying this.

One will find that what is given as the primary object of proteraesthesis is not directly a past quality and a past spatial determination thereof, but rather a past experience of the quality with its spatial determination.

One might be tempted to deceive oneself about this in the case of motion [or] change. However, I believe that in the case of rest everyone will, under careful self-examination, be able to notice that actually it is not directly the quality which appears as past, but one's experience.

97|98   (In [the case of] vision [this is] more [so] than in [that of] hearing, | because there [there is] more noticeable unrest. Look at your hand and recognize that it is at rest.)

So it seems that the primary object of proteraesthesis does not, properly [speaking], adjoin as continuation [*als Fortsetzung anschliessen*] the primary object of sensation, but rather something belonging to the secondary object, namely the intentional relation to the primary object which we call experience. Whereas sensation shows a present experiencing as its secondary object, proteraesthesis shows, as its primary object, a past experiencing which in its object matches the primary object of the preceding sensation.

We thus observe that the realization of the primary object of proterosis and its deviation from that of sensation is indeed considerable and needs to be marked clearly and precisely. All of this serves to recommend this, albeit merely fictitiously, isolating way of looking at sensation.

The question [whether temporal determination constitutes a third generally pervading part of primary objects] may at present not yet be decidable.

103

14. By allowing ourselves for these reasons to separate sensation and proteraesthesis as different fundamental acts, we are left, as far as the common characteristics of the primary object are concerned, with just the union of quality and spatial determination as mutually pervading parts.

Further Parts of Fundamental Psychical Acts

1. In view of this plurality of parts in the primary object, we are now able to amend some of the earlier determinations concerning the relations to the primary object which are given in the fundamental acts.

2. At an earlier stage we already established with certainty, or at least with great probability, that each fundamental psychical act has at least two intentional relations to the primary object: presenting and believing.
     So two parts arise in a certain way in this context.

98|99   3. As a result of the investigations we have just concluded which did allow us to discern a plurality of mutually ¦ pervading parts in the primary object of every fundamental psychical act, we are now forced to admit the possibility of distinguishing furthermore a plurality of mutually pervading parts in every fundamental psychical act. For, corresponding to the parts of the intentional objects, there are parts of the psychical acts directed at them. If, for example, in the case of seeing, colour and spatial determination pervade one another in the object, then we must accordingly distinguish in it [the seeing] the seeing of place [*das Ortsehen*] and the seeing of colour [*das Farbsehen*] as two mutually pervading parts.
     The seeing of the spatial determination and the seeing of the colour are, like spatial determination and colour, different genera.

4. This explains an [apparent] paradox which seems to establish that the law for the relations of logical parts is invalid in the case of sensation and other psychical acts.

Seeing = experiencing of colour.
Seeing-red – – seeing-blue.
Seeing-red here – – seeing-red there.
Seeing-blue here – – seeing-blue there.

(The last difference does not contain the previous ones.)

The solution is that we are here not dealing with successive specific differences of the same genus, but with different pervading parts.

5. So much concerning what all fundamental psychical acts have in common with regard to their relation to the primary object. As it was necessary to discuss this at somewhat greater length, we shall be all the more brief in the discussion of the relation of the fundamental acts to the secondary object. All we need to say is that the previously made general points about psychical acts remain valid in this case, in that they show at least a two fold relation to the primary object.

(1) presenting,
(2) non-evident assertoric believing.

Anything else which ought to be said in this context follows directly from this in conjunction with the results which have just been gained. 99|100   We do not need explicitly to identify it in detail . . . ¦

Other Opinions

1. Are the mentioned determinations really universal for all fundamental acts?

Yes, [this is] as certain as [the fact that] they consist only of sensations and proteraestheses. And this point seems to me completely secured, even though it is by no means unanimously recognized.

(a) Kantians [refer to] *a priori* intuitions of an infinite space and an infinite time. [They] furthermore [refer to] *a priori* universal concepts: being, not-being, necessity, possibility, substance and inherence, cause and effect, etc.

   Some [put forward] innate concepts of God.
(b) Empirical presentations of fantasy [are meant to be] fundamentally different from experiences ([the latter are] to be distinguished from fantastic sensory phenomena, [and] hallucinations).

   Moreover, [many believe that] the presenting of general concepts taken from experience is dependent on sensations and proteraestheses only in [its] acquisition but not in [its] continued

105

existence, in the way in which secondary acts [are dependent in their continued existence] on the fundamental ones.

(c) Many have also spoken of the existence of a will without presentation; [if this were the case, then] naturally the requirement for sensation and proterosis as foundations of will would be even more diminished.

2. Yet all these views are wrong.

I would be unfaithful to my earlier intention if I were to refute them in detail. But it seems that a few brief comments may be unavoidable.

3. [We do not have *a priori* concepts or infinite intuitions:]

(1) We do not have infinite intuition of space, [or] pure intuition of · space. We only have a concrete intuition of space tied to qualities, namely in the expansion of our phenomenal sensory fields. A different part [is relevant] for colours than for tones, and for these [yet another] than for smells etc.; otherwise [we would have] abstract spatial determinations.

100:1   Abstract concepts of spatial relations, in ¦ conjunction with numerical magnitudes and negative determinations, are in this context sufficient in serving to form unintuitive presentations of spaces of arbitrary, indeed infinite magnitude.

(2) The case is similar for time. The intuitive timespan of proterosis contains the relation of earlier and later. Everything else, including the future, arises from this in an unintuitive manner. The case is again similar to the alleged *a priori* or innate concepts.

(3) The concept of God.

(4) Being = existence. Correlate to the truth of the accepting judgment.

(5) Not-being = correlate to the truth of the negative judgment.

(6) Necessity and impossibility [as] correlates to the truth of apodeictic affirmative and negative judgments.

(7) From this [follows the] impossibility [of these supposedly *a priori* concepts].

(8) Substance and inherence [as] relation between mutually pervading parts, of which one is regarded as [being] the principal one; [for example] looking at physical concreta [or] the I. (Maybe in this case particularly, since the individuality [of the substance as such continues to exist] whereas accidents [occur and disappear].)

(9) Cause and effect. Cases of motivation etc.

106

4. The true nature of general concepts. The error of DESCARTES and LOCKE took revenge in the form of a nominalistic set-back. BERKELEY, HUME, CONDILLAC, MILL, etc.

5. The true nature of fantasy images.[32]

(a) [They have an] intuitive core.
(b) Supplementary [ergänzende] and correcting determinations exist productively [in their case].

6. Will without presentation [is] a clear absurdity or an equivocal use of the term 'will', similar to when one hears in everyday life:

'it wants to fall',
'it does not want to bend',
'it does not want to break', etc.

And much more often one hears of a 'striving' etc. (tendency) as applied to inanimate objects:

'The stone strives towards the deep',
101|2   'the arrow strives towards its target', |
'the power fails',
'the body in motion has the tendency to move in a straight line',
etc.

All these [statements] are allegories, be it that they came into being at the time of a vitalistic Weltanschauung (as still held by little children), or be it that they are consciously used in a metaphorical manner (as [in the case of] chemical affinity, elective affinity [Wahlverwandtschaft], fight for survival of plants, natural breeding choice, etc.).

It is left to a philosopher to commit the absurdity which neither the fetishist nor the one who, being conscious of the metaphor, applies the term 'will' to non-presenting things [nicht Vorstellendes] is guilty of, namely to teach the existence of a will in the proper sense without presentation.

7. Result: We keep our earlier list. [There are] no fundamental psychical acts apart from sensation and the accompanying proter-aesthesis. [There is] therefore no [fundamental psychical act] which does not display the mentioned characteristics.

Further Classes of Fundamental Acts

1. The fundamental acts fall into several classes. These can be formed from different points of view. One can classify fundamental acts in a first instance by considering agreement or difference in the primary object, and then by considering agreement or difference in the secondary object.

2. Concerning the first relation, the division into sensation and proteraesthesis, which we have already come to know, is of particular importance.

3. But there is yet another division regarding this first relation which could generally be carried out. Namely [the division] according to the primo-primary object – if I may coin the term.

In sensation the primo-primary object simply coincides with the primary object. In proteraesthesis the primo-primary object is different from the primary one ¦ and only contained in it in the [sort of] inessential [*uneigentlich*] way in which the parts gained (distinguished) through modifying distinction are contained in their whole. For example, in the case of visual proteraesthesis the having-seen a coloured object is the primary object; the coloured object in question is the primo-primary one.

The main classification of fundamental acts according to the primo-primary object is a division according to the number (differences) of senses. That is to say, according to the differences of the genera of the sensory qualities or, in HELMHOLTZ's terminology, according to the modalities of the primo-primary objects.

This classification clearly cuts across the previous one.

4. In regard to the secondary object, the most important classification is that into purely noetic and epithymetic acts, i.e. acts of the character of affect:

These are fundamental acts in which the subject stands in an intentional relation to the secondary object not only by presenting and evidently accepting, but also through an emotion.

We have already noticed that this is not generally the case. There is also nothing which, from the outset, would prevent this classification from cutting across the two earlier ones. For example, sensation as well as proteraesthesis [contain] partly noetic acts, partly affects; and similarly [we find that] auditory as well as visual and olfactory experiences etc. are partly noetic acts, partly affects.

5. In any case, it appears to be more suitable, as far as the structuring of the investigation is concerned, to consider as fundamental primarily the classifications with regard to the primary object, and of these in the first instance the classification into sensation and proteraesthesis.

6. Having adopted this last classification as being more basic than any of the others, and having established the general character of fundamental acts, let us now talk about the general character of 103¦4 sensations. ¦

3

THE GENERAL CHARACTER OF SENSATIONS

SPATIAL DETERMINATION [RÄUMLICHKEIT]

Introduction

1. Sensations differ from proteraestheses above all in virtue of a difference in primary objects.

We said that what fundamental psychical acts have in common is their primary object being [either] a concretum [composed] of spatial determination [*Örtlichkeit*] and something which takes up the place, or an analogue to such a concretum. [For] sensations, it is always the first of these alternatives which obtains.

2. Of the two mutually pervading parts which generally belong to every primary object of a sensation, let us first look at the spatial determination.

Every primary object of a sensation shows itself spatially. The meaning of this can easily be made intelligible with examples. When I open my eyes, I am usually confronted with a great diversity of visible [things]. Sometimes I see light and dark [things], red and blue [ones], yellow and white [ones], etc. At other times, the diversity is smaller, and I could imagine the case that everything I saw appeared to me equally light and equally coloured. Yet, in thus imagining as many differences as possible being removed, there would necessarily still remain some differences. Indeed, they [the remaining differences] would be virtually infinite in number, even though all of them turn out to be specific differences of one genus. This genus is spatial determination.

I could have used an example from any other sensory domain.

If, instead of visual phenomena, I were to use phenomena of

temperature, smell or hearing, and imagined them to be evened out as far as possible, then there would still remain certain differences which would be specific differences of the genus spatial determination.

104¦5   And when I speak of spatial determination in the context of colour, smell and sound phenomena, then I am not using ¦ the term ambiguously, but rather in completely the same sense.

3. However well we may know the genus of spatial determination, and however easily we may understand each other when we use the term, it will still be advisable to pause for a short while and examine its peculiarities.

4. Spatial determination is a genus with species that can only have continued existence [*Bestand haben*] (in reality as well as in intuition) as boundaries, in fact, as boundaries demarcating [*begrenzen*] something three-dimensional. Yet themselves they are without dimensions (extension).

Boundaries which do not have dimensions (extension) are called points in the widest sense of the word ([i.e. in the sense] in which one could equally well speak of temporal points, spatial points and points of the intuitive presentation of an extended magnitude).

General Points About Continua

1. Boundary point and continuum are inseparable concepts. Every continuum consists of nothing but boundary points. And each boundary point is nothing except in continuity with a host of other boundary points.

The curious thing is that each boundary point is not only specifically different but also specifically distanced [*spezifisch abstehen*] from every other boundary point in the continuum. That is to say, the specific difference between any two points of a continuum has a magnitude, indeed a definite finite magnitude. But none the less they form a continuity which might not display a gap anywhere.

2. Paradoxes!

(a) A magnitude out of nothing but zeros!
(b) Each distanced from every other, and yet all connected!

[It might be possible to find a] resolution [of these paradoxes by showing] how this can, and indeed actually does obtain in the case of the (continuous) number sequence (including the irrational and transcendental numbers).

105:6 Explanation: It cannot be shown [how] out of nothing but nothing- ness something can come into being, but [it can be explained] ¦ how a plurality can arise out of unities, even though no unity is a plurality.

It is furthermore curious that [it is] not just each continuum [which contains] infinitely many points, but also every separable part (indeed, even [some] inseparable ones, like surfaces, [or] lines, themselves [being] merely boundaries). Can something be more than the absolutely infinite? Or isn't the whole bigger than the part?

3. Possibility of a universal pair-wise coordination in a mutually exhaustive way [i.e. a one-one and onto mapping, or 'equivalence' in the set-theoretical sense] of the points of an arbitrarily small part of a dimension with the points of the whole. Illustration [by means] of concentric circles.

Similarly, it can be shown that the coordination is possible between the points of a line and those of a surface etc.

4. It is also possible to give a unique and mutually exhaustive pair-wise coordination between the point set of a continuum and the full set of integers.

I only mention this here in passing, for the fact can actually be treated with indifference in the present context. And anyway, after all you have just heard about possible coordinations, most of you will hardly be inclined to doubt this.

Yet certain scolars who have keenly occupied themselves in this domain, such as, in particular, CANTOR[32a] have denied this, but they are wrong. The simplest proof for this is [as follows:] through [successive] imagined bisection of a line [segment] one would arrive at a sequence of [bisection] points. Nowhere in the whole of this sequence would there be a distance between the points which would not be smaller than any one that could be given. The distance [between the points] would hence not have a finite magnitude, i.e. it would not have a magnitude at all. Rather [there would be] full continuity.[32b]

The set of points [*Punktmenge*]* of a continuum is thus to

---

* Even though I have chosen to translate '*Menge*' as 'set' throughout, it should be pointed out that in German this term can also mean 'quantity'.

be coordinated with a set of units which can be expressed by the formula:

$$1 + 2 + 4 + 8 \ldots in\ inf.$$

And of such a set it can easily be shown, and is generally accepted, that it can be uniquely pair-wise coordinated with a set of units

106:7   expressable by the formula: ¦

$$1 + 1 + 1 \ldots in\ inf.$$

Irrationality [of numbers] (like transcendentality etc.) loses its meaning in the infinite).

5. And so what do we answer to the questions raised and the calls of astonishment? Can something be more than what is infinitely manifold or is the whole not bigger than the part?

The correct answer is that infinite pluralities are magnitudes but not numbers because they cannot be counted but only measured in a different manner.

This measuring does not consist in a pair-wise coordination but results from considering the specific distances of the outermost [of the] boundaries ([the term] outermost is not appropriate in the case of bent [continua]) within which the continuum or the continua (if there are disruptions, gaps) formed by them are situated. For example, the set of spatial points [*Raumpunktmenge*] in a cubic foot is twice smaller than the one in two cubic feet. Furthermore, the set of spatial points in a cube without the boundary surfaces is smaller than with them, because all the remaining boundaries are less distanced from one another. Yet the convergence [between the two sets] is [so] great that their ratio could not be expressed by any fraction with finite pluralities as numerator and denominator. There is also no actual separability. (The question [remains] whether [this is] so only in presentation.)

6. Tied to this is, amongst other things, the important consequence that infinite point sets of different genera are not comparable in magnitude, [that they are] neither equal nor unequal sets.

7. Moreover, [it follows] that the same is true of completely abstract

infinite sets; they are neither equal nor unequal. This is why HELMHOLTZ, in the case of the square, multiplied named [items] [*Benanntes*] with named [ones]. Objection: Can one not say, between 0 and 5 are half as many numbers than between 0 and 10, because the boundaries are twice as distanced? Answer: Yes! But in this case they are named numbers; for we are dealing with quantities of ¦ numerals (finite number species), [and] not quantities of arbitrary units.

107¦8

8. Everything we have discussed so far was about points and continua in general.

And we must continue this discussion to be able to apply it later to what we are particularly concerned with here, [namely] the spatial, and to understand its special peculiarities.

9. Let me, in particular, mention that there are continua *per se* and continua *per accidens*.

The former are continua in the proper sense [of the word]. An example will straight away clarify the difference.

Think of the phenomenon of an evenly red disc. In this case, a continuum *per se* is formed by the spatial species; the colour which covers them forms a continuum *per accidens*.

In this case there are not infinitely many colour species realized (like the infinitely many spatial species); but only one.

10. Continua *per se* divide furthermore into necessary and not necessary ones.

A necessary one, for example, is time. Temporal species cannot exist other than as temporal points of a continuum.

A not necessary one, for example, would be a continuously rising tone; because even though here the individual tone species exist as the boundaries of a continuum, they could also, each by itself, exist alone as a mere continuum *per accidens*.

Another example of a not necessary continuum *per se* would be [given in] the case of a continuous sequence of colours in a plane such that every colour species were represented in a point.

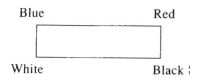

Blue   Red

White   Black ¦

108¦9

At this point we do not wish to investigate whether something like this could happen.

11. Examples like the ones just mentioned, can easily be used to clarify the difference between double continua (and indeed multiple continua) and simple ones. The case of a tone which continues to sound unchanged in time is that of a simple one. The case where it rises continuously is a case of a double continuum. If we assume that it changes continuously in time not just as concerns quality but also as concerns peculiarity [*Eigenheit*] (say, for example, if intensity were such [a peculiarity]), then one could speak of a threefold continuum *per se*.

Similar things hold for the example of colours.

12. But for each of these multiple continua one [of the component continua] is the primary one which only makes possible the continuity of the others. Like, for example, time in the case of the rising tone, [and] space in the case of the varying colour.
13. Important peculiarities are tied to the difference as to whether a continuum is primary or secondary. But it will be better to concern ourselves with them at a later stage.[33]

14. Another important difference of continua is that some only possess one, others several dimensions.

This fact is well known and very familiar to all of you. You will hardly demand that I define the concept and explain the differences by means of examples. But, I would be justifiably reproached if I omitted to add a few words of clarification so as to exclude certain errors which are sometimes made.

For it often happens that even scientific researchers (psychologists, physiologists, indeed mathematicians) misuse the name of dimension by calling a whole a continuum of several dimensions just because it consists of several pervading parts each of which displays a particular continuity. This is definitely reprehensible and must lead to conceptual confusion.

For example, if one attributes three dimensions to something spatial in virtue of being spatial and one dimension to time and then wants to attribute four dimensions to a body which exists for a period
109|10 of time. |

In the same manner one could attribute four dimensions to a plane surface covered with colours in the above-mentioned fashion by attributing two [dimensions] because of the change in spatial [species] of the plane, [and] two [dimensions] because of the change of colour species.

We are dealing here with species of different genera. We thus have two continua *per se* of two dimensions each. In order to speak of a four-dimensional continuum, all the varying species would have to be of the same genus.

If there is an actual plurality of dimensions, then the magnitude of the distances in one and another dimension can be compared. They [these distances] are equal, greater or smaller. This is not true for the said alleged multiplicity of dimensions of a continuum. Because the distances belong to [species of] different genera they do not have proportions of magnitude, according to previous elaborations.

15. Since this sort of error concerning the determination of the number of dimensions does occur, I wish to provide some short and clear definitions.

In order to make them understandable, let us recall that each continuum consists of continua which are connected by inner boundaries.

(a) Now, if these inner boundaries are, without exception, only (individual) points, then the continuum has one dimension. We may call it a line in the widest sense of the word, i.e. in a sense similarly wide as that of the term point when applied to spatial and temporal items, indeed to any extensionless boundary of a continuum regardless of its genus (continuum of first power).

(b) If the continuum also contains without exception (and all over) inner boundaries which themselves are continua of one dimension, then it has two dimensions. We could call it a surface in the widest sense of the word (continuum of second power).

(c) If it also contains without exception inner boundaries which are continua of two dimensions, then it has ¦ three dimensions. Extending the meaning of the term accordingly, we could call the continuum a three-dimensional space (continuum of third power).

(d) If it contains without exception inner boundaries which are continua of n-1 dimensions, then it is a continuum of n dimensions (continuum of n-th power).

110|11

16. This leads to the discussion of a further important classification of continua, namely into straight and curved [*gerade und ungerade*]

ones. [These are] expressions which are often not correctly understood (apart from the fact that in some cases one prefers the term 'flat' for what I call 'straight').

Instead of the intricate determinations which are to follow, it seems [to be] sufficient and preferable [in many cases to simply state]: a continuum is straight if between every two of its inner boundary points there is a third one.

(a) A one-dimensional continuum is straight if between every two of its points there is a third one. (A straight continuum of first power, or a straight line in the widest sense.)

(b) A two-dimensional continuum is straight if between every two of its one-dimensional inner boundaries (which are not related like the parts of one and the same straight line) there is a third one. (A straight continuum of second power, [or] a surface-geometrically flat [*planimetrisch eben*] continuum in the widest sense.)

(c) A three-dimensional continuum is straight if between every two of its two-dimensional inner boundaries (which are not related like the parts of a plane) there is a third one. (A straight continuum of third power, or space-geometrically flat [*stereometrisch eben*] continuum, or a plane space in the widest sense.)

(d) An *n*-dimensional continuum is straight if between every two of its *n*-1-dimensional inner boundaries (which are not related like the parts of a straight continuum of *n*-th power) there is a third one. (A straight continuum of *n*-th power, a straight *n*-dimensional space in the widest sense.)

111!12 17. And now, after so many important classifications ! of continua in general, finally one more. The genera with species which can form continua can be divided into two classes: those with certain species which constitute natural extremes, and those which do not have such natural extremes.

This has the consequence that there are natural maxima of extension in the ones [of the first kind], magnitudes the exceeding of which would in effect amount to an absurdity. Whereas in the case of the others, an increase of extension over any given limit seems conceivable.

E.g., lightness of colours.

Black, white.

In the case of time, [or] that of a spatial line, this is different. *Nota*

118

bene: Someone might ask whether one may say that the distance between black and white, and the magnitude of the whole continuum of lightness is smaller, [indeed] incomparably smaller than, for example, an infinite future.

[As a point] in favour [one might put forward the view that]: the former has a beginning and an endpoint, i.e. it is a finite magnitude, whereas the later is an infinite one.

But no! According to [what has been said] earlier [we have]: distances in different genera, [and] point sets of different genera do not have proportions of magnitude.

Indeed, a pair-wise coordination between possibilities of lightness and the infinite species of the future would also be possible. For example, in the first hour a decrease from white to middle grey, in the second one [a decrease] to the middle of the distance between middle grey and black, etc. *in infinitum*. We are thus not forced to retract or restrict what we put forward earlier as being necessary because of the peculiar difference between genera just mentioned.

Let us now turn from these general considerations about continua to those [continua] which are our first concern, the spatial ones, in 112|13 order to apply what we have found. ¦

Applications to the Spatial Continuum

1. We divided continua into continua *per se* and continua *per accidens*.

The spatial continuum is always a continuum *per se* and the spatial point is always a point of a continuum *per se*.

2. We divided the continua into necessary and not necessary [ones]. From what has just been said we can conclude that spatial continua always belong to the first kind.

3. We spoke of double continua and of multiple continua in general. And we said that in these cases one continuum will have the character of the primary continuum, the others that of secondary ones.

The spatial continuum in the primary object of our sensations may possibly also occur in double continua. In these cases it always has the character of the primary continuum, [while] the other or [those occurring] in the others [have the character] of secondary [ones].

I am now only talking of what is given in sensation as abstracted from proteraesthesis. The conditions become more complicated in the case of the latter because of the occurrence of the continuum of time, which is never a secondary one. [Another question is] how, in consequence, local motion [*örtliche Bewegung*] shapes the conditions in the phenomenon.

4. We distinguished continua according to the numbers of dimension.

As is well known, some spatial continua are one-dimensional, some two-dimensional and some three-dimensional. It is to be noted in this context that the one- and two-dimensional ones, like points, are only possible as boundaries, by themselves they are nothing. Everything they are, they are only in connection with the third dimension, i.e. with the physically spatial. We said earlier that a spatial point never exists without a continuum. This must still be more precisely determined to the effect that it can never exist without connection to three-dimensional spaces. What is true of reality is also true of intuition. (Correlates can again not be without one another.)

Thus, if somewhere in our sensory intuition there seem to be only two dimensions, then we can nonetheless claim with certainty that 113!14 there is yet a third one, which may only be unnoticeable. | (Be it because it is small or constant or whatever else the reason may be.)

5. We have divided continua into straight and curved [ones]. The spatial boundaries which are continua are without doubt often curved. But what about three-dimensional space? It is always and necessarily a straight continuum, a space-geometrically flat continuum or, as one usually says, a flat space.

Our previous discussion makes it unnecessary for me to discuss again this term, which is often misunderstood, and sometimes ridiculed by ignorant people.

If it were not a flat space, then there could not be a straight line between two points. It was a mistake of HELMHOLTZ to change the concept of the straight line. HELMHOLTZ: 'The straight [is] the shortest [line] between two points'.[34]

(a) According to this [there would be] a threefold geometry: Euclidean, Over-Euclidean [and] Under-Euclidean. (Actually [the classification would] not [be] threefold, but [there would be] infinitely many Over- and Under-Euclidean ones.)

120

[His definition is] very impractical, because the old one could have been retained.

(b) [He is] not consistent [in his terminology], because he himself speaks of the 'flat three-dimensional space' in contrast to 'curved' three-dimensional spaces.

(c) The 'straight line' would possibly have different relations of positions [*Lagenverhältnisse*] between the parts (*Gestalt*) in different places. It would no longer at all be suited as the fundamental measure. We would all the same have to return to the 'straight line' in the sense of a third point being between any two points. ARISTOTLE: The straight line [is] the appropriate measure for itself and for the curved [one].

6. Finally, we have divided continua into those which have certain species with a widest conceivable distance from one another, and those where a widening of distances into the infinite is conceivable. Which [class] does the genus of space which occurs in the primary
114|15 objects of our sensations belong to? |

My answer is: the second one. In no dimension, in no direction are there species which are extreme according to their nature.

Yet this should not be misunderstood. *De facto* there are ultimate (extreme) species which our intuition cannot surpass.

But the unsurpassability is not given by the nature of the genus, but only by the factual limitation of our capacity to intuit, [by the limitations] of our sensory fields. The lack of any limitation due to the concept of the genus is as certain as the existence of limitations due to certain barriers of our consciousness. People have often deluded themselves into thinking that because the first [limitation] does not exist, the second does not either. [They thought] either we had an infinite *a priori* intuition of space, or that imagination has the gift to extend intuitively: colour-pictures towards the back etc.

No! The sensory field of tones cannot be filled [with non-auditory phenomena], not even with colour. If simultaneously all our nerves are appropriately stimulated, we will have a finite intuition of space that contains every point we can ever, in general, present intuitively.

7. Finally, the continuum is real; [it is] not like the temporal continuum merely delimited by something real which itself no longer partakes of the species of time.

We have thus far spoken of the spatial determination in the primary object. Let us now speak of what occupies the places.

OF WHAT FILLS SPACE

Light [*Hell*] and Dark [*Dunkel*]

1. The difference between light and dark is universal.

2. It is often to be understood in an identical, and often in a merely analogous sense. One can say that this colour is lighter than that one, that this tone is lighter* than that one, but not that this colour is lighter than that tone, or *vice versa*. Cool also is lighter than warm.

115:16   3. Where there is no unity of genus for light and dark, ¦ there is no common concept, but only the same relationships.

4. Accordingly, the differences are not distances, [or] magnitudes.

It is in this sense that HELMHOLTZ speaks of two degrees of differences,[35] [and this is a] most fundamental distinction. Otherwise HELMHOLTZ would contradict himself, for he correctly says: transitions are inconceivable, something in the middle between colour and tone is absurd. That is, [it would be absurd to say] that there is something between colour and tone, or, [for that matter,] something is closer to the one than the other. Hence, there is no distance, no magnitude [between colour and tone] as, for example, between high and low tones where there is a continuous connection.

5. We determine the number of senses according to the number of genera of light and dark.

6. If we imagine a phenomenal space to be filled with two sensory qualities of which the one is lighter than the other, [and if] both are mixed in a mixture so fine that no particle is noticeable by itself whereas the whole is noticeable, then we will attribute a medium lightness to the whole.

If we imagine the same space to be similarly filled with two sensory qualities of which the one is light in a different sense from the other etc. then we will not attribute a medium lightness to the whole, rather we would only be able to speak of a union of two qualities, of which we might be inclined to think that they, in

---

* In German both light colours and high-pitched tones are referred to as being 'hell', which, in view of Brentano's own unorthodox use of this term in the context of temperatures, I have chosen to translate throughout as 'light'.

penetrating one another, pervade the whole [of this] space. More-over, the presence of the one [lightness] would not be an obstacle to the recognition of the other lightness. Except [for] the weakening of the phenomenon due to the presupposed gaps.

7. In the phenomena of the visual sense we have extremes of lightness and darkness, black–white.

This leads to the conjecture that the case is similar wherever we are dealing with lightness and darkness.

Yet here it must be striking that for tones the contrary seems to be the case. Higher and lower [tones] *in infinitum* seem to be con-ceivable without absurdity, even if we cannot hear them, ¦ nor produce them intuitively in fantasy (subjective experience). Without noticing, one falls into repetitions of the previous octave. And by themselves they seem to be able to rise and sink *in infinitum*. Yet a closer investigation reveals a curious deception.

116¦17

The distances of the octaves are not equal. They are greatest in a certain middle [range], going up and down they decrease in a way such that [even if they were] continued in infinitum no infinite distance would result.

Thus, there is no obstacle to assuming what the analogy [to the visual sense] demands, indeed it is in a way reinforced. And so we may, I believe, claim very confidently that it is a universal fact for all genera of lightness that they have natural extremes (even though they may not, and certainly not purely by themselves, be noticeably given in our experience).

Colouredness [*Kolorit*] and Non-colouredness [*Nicht-Kolorit*]

We are now considering the difference between coloured and not coloured (colourless), tonal and toneless and analogues (saturation and noise).

(a) That which fills space in the primary objects of visual experience not only displays the difference between light and dark, but also other [differences] at the same lightness: coloured, colourless, red-coloured, blue-coloured, etc. How do they relate to light and dark?

These differences are often called qualitative differences.

(b) Accordingly, it seems that one is dealing with one genus. In this manifold different directions. The genus would be something which in the totality of its species could be represented like a continuum of several dimensions.

(c) Yet this view is questionable.

    (1) Common language use already distinguishes coloured and colourless in the manner of something privative. This may also be the case for evident and ¦ blind believing and accepting, but it is not so for a unity of genus [which has] several dimensions.

    (2) There would have to be an axis which is particularly distinguished in the multidimensional continuum. Yet this seems curious, and the distinction can probably only be understood in a casual manner by saying that [in the distinguished axis] every species presents only a degree of lightness, and nothing more, whereas [elsewhere] there is yet something else involved.

(d) While the above view could scarcely be upheld, someone else might think it correct to assume throughout, apart from spatial determination, two further mutually penetrating parts.

    (1) The quality in the sense of the genus whose differences [are] light and dark, [and]

    (2) the quality in the sense of the genus whose differences are blue, red, yellow, black, etc.

(e) But this too would, presumably, be an error.

    (1) According to this, it would be conceivable that [(a) one and] the same lightness or darkness [could occur] in any colour, [and (b) that one and] the same colour [could occur] in any lightness or darkness. Yet it seems that a colour which is pure [possesses] nothing but a [single] lightness.

    (2) To assume pure white and pure black in different lightness would be obvious non-sense. Furthermore, it would be nonsense [to assume] that two, three or n other species be as light as white, [or] as dark as black. This [is] only [possible] because pure lightness–darkness [is assumed].

    (3) Hence this second view is also to be rejected.

(f) In order not to continue any longer to put forward and criticize untenable opinions, [let me state the following].

    (1) The only correct view is presumably that two genera [are] to be distinguished. The one is lightness and darkness; it is in every visual phenomenon. The other is colouredness, saturation or however one may call it, which is sometimes present and sometimes missing, like evidence in the case of judgment.

    (2) The most common [of these] expressions, [namely] coloured–

colourless, thus appear to be quite appropriate and show how in the course of experience the correct conception has forced itself even on non-psychologists (even though no clear justifying account [¦ is given by them]).

118¦19

(3) Someone might ask: how then [can there be] whitish yellow and non-whitish yellow? [And] is whitish red light [*hell*] [in the same sense] as pure yellow, given that anything light, *qua* being light, appears white?

This question will be answered without contradicting what has already been said as soon as we have become clear about the true nature of multiple qualities. Of this more at a later stage.[36]

(g) Earlier, I have on occasion mentioned a different view, according to which it is [actually] a difference in emotions (affects) [– and] not [a difference in] the primary object of sensation [–] which gives rise to the division of sensations into coloured and colourless ones.

[This is] certainly not so! Powerful emotions are tied also to black-grey as colour of mourning etc. if it is used for emotional effect; black purity [has a] particular emotional effect in combinations of other [colour tones].

(h) Let us call the one genus [that of] colour lightness (visual modality), [and] the other [one], which is only added sometimes, [that of] visual colouredness or colour quality in the strict sense.

(i) Again we are led to the conjecture that it will be analogous with the other sense. And indeed, looking at the domain of tones we see nothing contradictory . . .

We can say that what we have found for the visual sense is also [true] for the auditory sense:

First [there is] a genus whose differences are the differences of lightness and darkness, so-called height–depth, and it is always given.

Then [there is] a second genus analogous to the distinguishing peculiarity of colours in the narrower sense: sounds in the narrower sense. This [does] not [apply to] completely unsaturated noises.

Nota bene: In the same way in which a colour species occurs pure only in one lightness, a tone species (presumably) occurs

119¦20

pure at only one height. ¦

Objection: [There are] many C, higher ones – deeper ones. We seem to contradict what we have just said. Answer: We also speak

125

of light blue and dark blue. (The mixing in of white (or grey) or black.) Vowels and other tone colours show how intimate such a mixing in can be for tones.

In the deeper octave one notices the veiling of the tones through a kind of tonal black, in the high ones through a tonal white. This explains as [being] a necessary consequence the shrinking of the octave in depth and height (as with colour distances).

From the outset, unsaturated, simple middle lightnesses between the extremes would [also] be conceivable. They too could be placed beside coloured qualities of tones and thus explain the lesser saturation of the higher and deeper [tones], if one were to assume that the mixed-in unsaturated lightness increases quantitatively towards the extremes.

(k) Now, [given that] the situation for tones is the same as that for colours, it is probably not bold of us to say that one can claim with a high probability that this is a general state of affairs for all sensory domains.

Summary

1. That which fills space in sensation,[37] that which takes up space, which is tied to spatial determination as another pervading part, is thus always something belonging to the genus of light and dark, and often something which has saturation (colouredness), which [itself] is to be understood as a third pervading part. The concept here is again not uniform, there is merely an analogy between the different senses.

2. However, it seems to me that with these three pervading parts the number of pervading parts, in the primary object of experience is, in 120:1 any case, exhausted. We have no reason to assume a fourth one. :

APPENDICES

Appendix I

INNER PERCEPTION*

Is it possible for us to perform a psychical activity without it falling into our inner perception? Many have claimed this to be the case. (Philosophy of the unconscious.) Others, who are themselves worthy, have denied it. Yet that view is not completely wrong in the sense of not touching upon any truth at all. (Only it was not the philosophy of the unconscious which first revealed this truth.)

Everything psychical falls under inner perception. But this does not mean that everything is noticed.

It is implicitly but not explicitly presented and perceived.

Explanation:

To present distinctly, to occupy oneself [with something] is not something second, and removed; it is, however, in many respects as good as something removed, serving as a basis, in particular, for judgments and emotions.

Another time [the presenting is] indistinct. At this point I shall only say as much as is required to clarify what we are dealing with, and to lead to the conviction that such a fact really does occur, yet is not given with inner perception.

Example: a little speck like a lark is seen yet not noticed. It is not noticed as part of the content of experience, [i.e. as] object of inner perception.

This circumstance [is] a second reason why descriptive psychology might be imperfect in spite of the evidence of inner perception. Because, to perceive [something] implicitly is obviously not sufficient for a description, [for this] it must be noticed. Yet this happens only under certain conditions (with attention, itself a rather vague concept).

121|2   In certain cases noticing is difficult, or cannot be achieved at all. |

* From the lectures of 1887–8.

1. Certain parts (logical or metaphysical ones) are only [noticed] if one moment [they] are given, and the next they are not; or if one moment they are tied to this difference, and the next to that one. For example, colour and blue are not noticed in a particular difference if blue is the only colour.

The intensity of tones is likewise not [noticed] if all [the tones] are equally loud. And it is not just the genus and the difference of the existing intensity which will not be noticed at all, but also the intensity as differing from the qualities.

If [the intensity] really [were] unnoticed, then one could only conclude that either

(a) it really is not present, or
(b) it is in fact present, but completely or almost constant.

And the latter of these assumptions would then be incomparably more probable.

2. Let me point out yet another class of cases with complete unnoticeability of a perceived part (qualitative unnoticeability just because one uses 'almost'):

(a) smallness of spatial extension according to HUME's scruple;[38]
(b) shortness of time (as good as impossible, at least for all practical purposes, even if theoretically possible). God could create a human being in the state of attending to a certain part or trait. Also, the object which has been distinctly perceived is always [noticed] from the first moment onwards;
(c) a very low degree of intensity;
(d) a very low degree of the qualitative peculiarity referred to as a 'tint of red' etc. Analogues presumably in all circles of experience [. . .];
(e) very small differences in spatial or temporal magnitude, or [very small differences of] distances of intensity, of the degrees of the tint of red, of height, of lightness etc.: 'thresholds'.

3. There are still other cases where noticing is partly made impossible, partly more difficult.

Amongst them are the ones where a multitude of differences
122!3   coincide in different respects. !

Mind you, [the fact that] that there really is a distinction [*Unter-*

schied] between two things which differ in virtue of many differences, will in fact be more easily recognized than if there were only one [difference], in particular if none of [the differences] alone is very important.

[This can lead to a] veiling [*Verschleierung*] of, for example, strength, height and quality (tone colour). Yet it is less a veiling of that which is the distinction between them; in particular if, apart from this distinction, there are other aspects in which important distinctions [between them occur], such as, for example, a difference of intensity in the case of tones of different heights; or [of] height in the case of tones of different tone colour ([it often happens that one] is wrong by two octaves); or [of] lightness in the case of different colours (for example, if grey is as light as pure red or pure yellow); intensity of different smells or tastes; intensity of warmth and coolness, of temperature and touch, and of taste and tone.

There is a dispute whether intensities in the case of different quality circles, indeed in the case of different species of qualities, can be the same at all, or [whether, like] the magnitudes of time and space, [they cannot be compared].

[This dispute is] certainly an indication of the magnitude of the difficulties for noticing arising from these circumstances.

The threshold, in any case, is considerably higher. There is the tendency to take the higher tone for being louder and *vice versa*.

Nota bene: Accompanying feelings and concomitant experiences can also belong to the veiling conditions.

4. Another case of particular difficulty which deserves to be emphasized is:

We have several phenomena of the same genus, and we notice a difference between the first and the second, and between the second and the third[; between] these differences there is itself again a relationship of agreement or difference.

This can often be noticed, and often it is. Yet in most cases the matter is much more difficult, for example whether differences in heights of tones agree with, or differ from, a third middle tone. And even more so, whether in the case of four tones ¦ there are differences between any of the pairs and the other one.

123¦4

The same is true in all domains.

In many cases this might simply be the result of the fact that, even though the first foundations are very different, the relationships are

131

not much different, such that the difference lies below the threshold. Yet in other cases this is not sufficient.

It rather seems to be the result of the necessarily bigger complication [given in] a certain division of attention, which makes noticing more difficult.

5. Yet another case in which noticing is often made extraordinarily difficult, indeed almost impossible, is the one of the absorption of attention by something else.

Everyone knows that an object often draws the attention, as one says, from another one, such that little or nothing is noticed of it. At some point one will presumably draw one's attention back to it; but in doing so one will precisely draw one's attention away from the other one. It is part of the nature of these objects that one cannot at all, or only in a very imperfect way, attend to both of them simultaneously. This sort of incompatibility of attention can also occur between phenomena which exist simultaneously, and of which one is such that it draws more interest. As a result of this, the other one will often not at all be noticed, and often it cannot be noticed no matter how much effort one exerts (by having been led through inferences to suspect the existence of this phenomenon). The blind spot was not noticed before MARIOTTE[38a]

6. The circumstance that the one draws more interest than the other may sometimes be given by nature, and sometimes it may spring from habit. Interesting tones (colours) will, in the case of a musician (painter) absorb the attention more (more easily). Habitual neglect of noticing a certain phenomenon can, as many famous psychologists and physiologists teach us, make this phenomenon completely unnoticeable (HELMHOLTZ's local signs [*Lokalzeichen*]). It is curious 124|5 that all the same they should attain | a decisive influence as signs. Yet this paradox at least is no reason for a rejection.

If this case is not certain, then other cases are, where signs which tell us something very interesting, while in and for themselves they are not very attractive, remain unnoticed but nonetheless provide the relevant instruction. For example, experiences instructing us about the position of our limbs. [Yet about this there are] disputes even amongst scientists, and they conduct experiments (such as skinning) to gain knowledge indirectly.

Nature and habit often work together. And who would wish to deny that they can bring about a completely immovable obstacle for any effort [*Schwierigkeit des Bemühens*] [to notice]?

7. Another frequent obstacle to noticing is the prejudice that something does not exist. For example:

(a) in the case of black, [the prejudice] that there is no experience (because there is no stimulus [*Erreger*]);
(b) in the case of the blind spot, where many scientists are meant to have arrived at, so to speak, perceiving that there is a gap, and hence at recognizing that they do not experience anything there. [. . .]

A very complex prejudice [is given in the assumption that a simple name stands for a simple concept]. One is of the opinion that the presentation itself must be simple and fails to notice anything of its complexity. This is so for red, green, etc., or for God where many believe that it is a simple concept because he has been associated with the idea [*Vorstellung*] of a simple being.

Based on linguistic expression there is a prejudice about the nature of judgments.

8. We have seen how there can be cases where habit increases the difficulty of noticing.

There are other cases where novelty carries with it particular difficulties.

Novelty has a particular appeal.

Something which nature particularly absorbs through attention will therefore often be particularly strongly [absorbed] in the presence of the appeal of novelty. Only through repeated experiencing will one succeed in noticing what is thus obscured. The noticing makes progress and grasps the insignificant components. |

125|6

What novelty lacks is, in particular, the practice in noticing, and it has been decided that the capacity [to notice] grows through practice (WEBERian experiments).

One and the same individual gets different results during frequent repetitions (*Nota bene*: particularly [in repetitions] of this specialty [*Spezialität*]) and notices differences which earlier he did not notice.

9. A different impediment lies in fatigue. (One could conclude from this that it is particularly difficult to study phenomena of fatigue.)

10. Similar things are certainly true of the moods of passion, for

133

example anger, which are incompatible with analysing observations. (Analysis within memory; yet [this can] even less [be] a substitute for an analysing noticing in the present [*Gegenwart*], because where there is no noticing, retainment is worse).

The same will presumably be also true of other cases!

All of this gives rise not only to deficiencies in descriptive psychology, insofar as gaps are concerned, but also to the dangers of errors, insofar as one is often misled to deny the unnoticed.

(a) We have seen this in the case of HUME's small parts of extension.
(b) We have seen this in the case of black.
(c) We find thousandfold that things are declared (and confused) as equal where a difference goes unnoticed (even though it is nothing less than [being] unnoticeably small), for example, the case of equivalent presentations of experiential contents.
(d) It is often denied that one can only compare indirectly, because consciousness does not notice anything of what mediates. As a consequence of this, an optimism arises which otherwise would not exist.
(e) The cases are particularly frequent where phenomena are taken to be equal although they are very unequal. They are merely equivalent signs [*Zeichen*] for one and the same third thing which is of particular interest. For example, in the case of looking at an object with a tilted position of the head. The vertical lines still appear to be seen vertically, the horizontal lines horizontally. The visual image appears unaltered, whereas it is in fact considerably different, but certain muscular experiences (or whatever else may further contribute) give an equivalent sign for the position of the object. [Another example is] touching of the forehead with a hand. Fingertips and hand appear with putatively the same spatial determination. But maybe it is more correct [to say] that so different impressions (such as the one given when the hand is stretched far away, and fingertips and forehead are pressed together) are always [impressions] of certain other experiences which serve them as an equivalent sign for an objective localization. Again this is only putatively so: two fingertips pressed together provide an almost indiscriminate experience. [This is our] first impression, because we habitually [believe that we are] dealing with two experiences directed towards an object. ARISTOTLE's experiment with the pellets.

126!7

There is a possible re-adaptation if the fingers are crossed for a long time. The deception is only increased.

Nota bene: The taking to be the same of what is not the same is in all these cases easily linked to a taking to be different of what is the same, like, for example [the taking to be different] of the impression of the tilted picture, or of the impression of the same fingertip if it is pressed [to the forehead] at different positions. (Has it not sometimes been said that the nerve always experiences the place of the peripheral ending, implying thus very different experiences depending on the position.) [. . .]

There is yet another disadvantage tied to the fact that, as we explained, not all that falls into inner perception will, just for that reason, also be noticed. If [the contrary] were the case then we would have everything at once.

Yet – given the great intricacy [and the] rich diversity [*Mannigfaltigkeit*] – we only have one after the other.

Impossibility of an attention to everything.

Thus, it is appropriate to check through, piece by piece, to collect in memory what is found, and to recognize the completeness inductively. It is quite clear that, in this case, the error [of incorrectly believing that] one already has an exhausting analysis is not excluded.

The evidence of inner perception, in any case, is no guarantee for
127¦8   it. ¦

We have come to know the reasons which complicate descriptive pychology.

(1) The temptation of mixing up and confusing very different phenomena.
(2) The not-noticing (which, in particular, also contributes to increase and augment this temptation).

In addition to this, there is a third reason which is linked to the task of providing measurements.

How incomplete the bodily anatomy would be without them. The same can be said of descriptive psychology, being, so to speak, the
128¦9   'anatomy of the soul'.[. . .] ¦

135

Appendix 2

DESCRIPTIVE PSYCHOLOGY OR DESCRIPTIVE PHENOMENOLOGY*

THE CONCEPT OF DESCRIPTIVE PSYCHOLOGY

1. By this I understand the analysing description of our phenomena.

2. By phenomena, however, [I understand] that which is perceived by us, in fact, what is perceived by us in the strict sense of the word.

3. This, for example, is not the case for the external world.

4. To be a phenomenon, something must exist in itself [*in sich sein*]. It is wrong to set phenomena in opposition to what exists in itself [*an sich Seienden*].

5. Something can be a phenomenon, however, without being a thing in itself, such as, for example, what is presented as such [*das Vorgestellte als solches*], or what is desired as such.[39]

6. One is telling the truth if one says that phenomena are objects of inner perception, even though the term 'inner' is actually super-fluous. All phenomena are to be called inner because they all belong to one reality, be it as constituents or as correlates.

7. By calling the description of phenomena descriptive psychology one particularly emphasizes the contemplation of psychical realities. Genetic psychology is then added to it as the second part of psychology.

---

* From the lectures of 1888–9.

8. Physiology has to intervene forcefully in the latter, whereas descriptive psychology is relatively independent of it.

9. Descriptive psychology is the prior part [of psychology]. The relationship between it and genetic psychology is similar to the one between anatomy and physiology.

10. *The value of descriptive psychology.*

(a) It is the foundation of genetic psychology.

129¦30 (b) It has a value in itself because of the dignity of the psychical domain. [. . .] ¦

THE GENESIS OF DESCRIPTIVE PSYCHOLOGY

1. It would be a mistake to believe that, because our phenomena are partly real, partly non-real, it is possible to divide [the subject matter] such as to talk first of the ones and then of the others. The knowledge of the correlatives is one.

2. If we wish to describe the psychical domain, we must first show how the objects of our psychical activities and the differences in the modes of relation are to be understood.

3. The order according to the differences of the objects is sufficient. And for this we will only have to take into account the objects of presentations.

4. The order will be an affiliation [*Angliederung*]:

(a) Description of the objects of our experiences,
(b) of our original associations,
(c) of our superposed presentations,
(d) of the presentations of our inner perception.

SUMMARY

1. I have briefly explained what I mean by descriptive psychology, and how it relates to genetic psychology and to psychology in

general. This was followed by some remarks concerning the value of descriptive psychology and its difficulties. I have also explained my views on the way in which I wish to deal with the subject, and, in particular, on the way in which I wish to take into consideration last year's lectures.

2. Descriptive psychology, we said, sets itself the task of an analysing description of our phenomena, i.e. of our immediate experiential facts [*Erfahrungstatsachen*], or, what is the same, of the objects which we apprehend in our perception. In tackling this task today, we must above all provide a division [of the subject matter] which can be decisive for the order of the investigations. By perceptions we understand only those [features] which deserve that

130¦1 name truly and properly, and this are only those ¦ which, in contrast to the so-called outer perceptions, are usually called inner perceptions. The objects of inner perception exist truly and in themselves; for example, our thinking, our joy and our pain exist in themselves. It is thus an error to put phenomena in opposition to what exists in itself. What is required above all for something to be a phenomenon is rather that it exists in itself. Mind you, it is, however, not necessary that something which is a phenomenon be a thing in itself. Indeed this is not the case for much of what belongs to phenomena. The realities which fall into our perception are psychical, i.e. they display an intentional relation, a relation to an immanent object.

These realities are not possible without a correlate; and these correlates are not real.

3. The domain which we are to describe thus displays real and non-real phenomena.

Now, someone might possibly believe that from this we can infer grounds for dividing up [our] investigations. We could, say, first speak of the real and then of the non-real phenomena (or *vice versa*). But one will soon recognize that this is imprudent. The knowledge of correlatives is one [i.e. indivisible].

4. The matter must thus be approached completely differently. If we compare different psychical activities together with their correlates amongst one another, we will find that between them there is a difference either with respect to the object to which they refer, or

139

with respect to the way in which they refer to it – in which case the difference can again be more or less profound and differentiated from various subordinate points of view. These two points of view are, in general, exhaustive; it can, however, also happen that differences occur simultaneously in both respects.

Examples:

imagine [*vorstellen*] a triangle,
wish for the luck of a friend.

5. If we want to describe a psychical activity, we will have to describe its particular object and the manner in which ¦ the activity refers to it. And if – according to the aims of descriptive psychology – we want to give a general description of the domain of our psychical activities, then we will have to show, in general, the nature of the objects of our psychical activities, and [the nature] of the differences of modes of relation in which we relate to them psychically.

It thus seems that we must take the difference of objects and the difference of modes of relation, one after the other, as decisive for the order of our investigation.

6. However, if we look more closely, we find that the order of the differences of objects is sufficient by itself.

This is so because the psychical relations and their differences themselves belong to the objects. Which is why an order according to objects can be fully sufficient for the whole.

7. In doing so we will only have to take the objects of presentations into consideration; for nothing can be an object of a psychical activity without at the same time being an object of a corresponding presentation.

8. Having said this, we shall order our description in the following manner: we give an analysing description

(a) of the objects of our experiences,
(b) of our original associations (or of our intuitive sensory mnemonic presentations [*sinnlich anschauliche Gedächtnisvorstellungen*]),

140

(c) of our superposed presentations (abstract presentations (concepts)),

(d) of the presentations of our inner perception.

The Presentations of Inner Perception

Another question which can be raised is whether the presentations of one's own hearing [*Vorstellungen vom eigenen Hören*], seeing, etc., which we have when we experience sounds, colours,
132!3 etc., belong likewise to the domain of experiences.¦

ARISTOTLE spoke of a [perception (ἐν παρέργῳ)].

And today, many people might still be inclined to say that if one hears a tone, one's own hearing is concomitantly experienced.

However, this accompanying presentation of hearing itself turns out [(a)] to be a presentation of inner perception, and [(b)] to be more closely related to the other presentations of inner perception (such as, for example, the presentation of one's own judging, or wanting etc.) than to the experiential presentations [*Empfindungsvorstellungen*] of colours and sounds.

Admittedly, the other presentations of inner perception have also been called presentations of the inner sense. And if sense and experience are used correlatively and thus sensory presentation is taken to be the same as experiential presentation, then this would indicate that one wishes to count them all as experiential presentations.

Yet this would really be drawing somewhat bold conclusions, and moreover misinterpreting the intention in a majority of cases. The term 'sense' has all too many equivocations (artistic sense, sense of justice). Why should it here not also be taken in a particular and, at most, analogous meaning?

At any rate, for the sake of clarity let me expressly say that we completely exclude from experiences the presentations which we have with the inner perception of our judging, our volition, etc. For them we have distinguished – as we may recall – a particular class [namely that of] (inner) perceptual presentations [*Wahrnehmungsvorstellungen*].

Experiences

[. . .]

Enough of the illustration of experiences by means of positive and negative examples.

If someone still desires a different analysis of the concept, then we can furthermore correctly say:

experience is a *fundamental presentation with real psychical* 133¦4 *content* [of real physical phenomena (objects)[39a]. [. . .] ¦

Appendix 3

OF THE CONTENT OF EXPERIENCES*

1. We begin our psychological analyses with the description of the content of experiences.

2. It will here above all be necessary to explain the concept of experiences and so to determine clearly the initially envisaged domain.

3. The need for this is all the more obvious given that with a little care it is easily noticeable that the term 'experience' is associated with a multiple concept.

One says

(a) I experience a colour, or a tone;
(b) I experience a yearning for it, a desire for it, joy about it or sorrow about it.

In the last case one could also have said: I am yearning for it, I am desiring it, I rejoice about it or I am sorry about it. Experiencing is thus used to describe an emotional activity. This is not so in the first case.

Whether the colour arouses pleasure or displeasure in me, whether I am interested or disinterested in it, is irrelevant.

Yet, the colour appears to me; I have a sensory presentation of it. This is an essentially different behaviour of the soul. Emotional activity, like presentation, is intentionally directed towards something. But the manner is a completely different one. There we have love or hatred, here neither of them: but [we have] presenting.

* From the lectures of 1887–8.

143

4. How little one tends to be clear, even so, about the big difference between the two meanings is shown by cases where we use the term experience uniformly for both; for example, 'I experience a pain in my foot'. We are dealing here with the expression of a sensory presentation of a certain quality located in the foot, yet at the same time certainly also with the aversion tied to the occurrence of this sensory presentation (which is an emotional activity not appearing as localized in the foot). ¦

134¦5

This is a dual usage and a mixture similar to the one for the word 'to feel', only that here the one (first) meaning does not stretch (reach) as far as the corresponding one of 'experiencing'.

5. Speaking now of experiences, we use the term in the first sense.

Thus, if we speak of the content of experience, we mean the content of certain presentations.

6. But of which presentations[?]!
The examples put forward, such as 'I experience a colour, or a tone' are not sufficient for a clarification.

For one, the presentations of colours and tones do not exhaust the domain, and then, not every presentation of colour or tone is an experience.

A generalization and a more precise statement are thus required.

7. We could say: experience is a sensory presentation. Yet this expression again is not free of ambiguity. One moment it is applied to a wider, the next to a more narrow circle of phenomena.

8. It could well seem doubtful whether the presentation of seeing itself, which we have while we experience colour, is to be counted as a sensory presentation. Many people have done this, and accordingly have spoken of an inner sense which they contrasted to the outer one. [. . .]

9. Again it could be doubtful whether the presentation of a tone in a melody, or of a colour, which appears to me as being recently past, is to be counted as a sensory presentation or not. (Phenomenon of original association.)

Many will affirm this.

Yet in this case the term 'sensory presentation' would again overstep the boundary of the domain which we wish to delineate.

Commonly one will also hardly say that one experiences a phenomenon of a tone which appears as being past.

10. How then are we to fix unambiguously what we understand by experience?

Many people are inclined towards a determination through the exciting cause. So, for example, FICK: [40] 'In the consciousness of a subject whose sensory nerve endings ! are stimulated a state occurs which we call an "experience"'; something which, as he emphasizes, is 'merely an object of inner intuition'. Indeed, this tendency is so widespread that SULLY,[40a] in his *Outlines of Psychology* (1885) bluntly declares: the meaning of

135!6

> 'experience, given that it is an elementary mental phenomenon, cannot be explained other than by reference to the nerve processes which one knows it to be dependent on. Accordingly, an experience will commonly be defined as a simple mental state resulting from the stimulation of the outer or peripheral ending of an inwardly conducting or sensitive nerve. The stimulation of a point of the skin through pressure or friction or of the retina through light thus gives rise to an experience.'

LOTZE too talks in just about the same manner.

11. Yet I have my reservations.

(a) I do not wish to raise as an objection the point that what is given here is only an outline and not a determination containing the essence of experiential presentations themselves.

This outline could still be indirectly of use in that it would allow us to multiply the illustrating cases. It would, for this reason, not even be objectionable in descriptive psychology, which *ex professo* is not concerned with the question of genesis.

(b) However, it [this outline] does seem to me to be too narrow.

The stimulation [*Reizung*] of the peripheral [nerve] ending is, as is being admitted, not the immediate stimulus.

A stimulation of nerves can also occur along the path [of the nerve].

[Examples:] Subjective experiences; hallucinations.

[These experiences and those peripheral ones] are, taken by

themselves, evidently homogeneous, indeed they are indiscernibly equal experiences.

This is why one commonly counts these [non-peripheral] experiences as experiences. And justifiably so; they do not form a separate class, in particular from the descriptive standpoint.

For the purpose of a widening [of SULLY's definition] one would thus have to insert something like:

136!7

'. . . [a simple mental state,] resulting from the stimulation of the peripheral ending of a sensitive nerve or from a brain process ! which is of the same kind as the one induced by the stimulation of the peripheral nerve ending.'

Yet this would be a very opaque determination, for our knowledge is not sufficient to describe with certainty the immediate physiological antecedents or (as many call it) the physiological substratum.

12. Someone might rejoin: in this case I shall help myself in a different way: I amplify with a different additional remark, namely

'. . . [a simple mental state,] resulting from the stimulation of the peripheral ending of a sensitive nerve, or one which is related to the ones resulting from such stimulations, and which in its character is similar to, or homogeneous with them; [i.e.] which does not differ from them more than they do amongst each other.'

13. Reservations [remain].

(a) The determination is obviously somewhat difficult to comprehend, but this does not mean that it is absolutely reprehensible.
(b) Other shortcomings which it displays are more serious. It can be considered to be certain that if consciousness is excited in us through a nerve stimulation, a plurality of psychical relations is given immediately in the first moment of consciousness. Moreover, the experience also contains pleasure or displeasure; furthermore a cognition [*eine Erkenntnis*] of the experience and a presentation of the experience as well as [a presentation] of this cognition.

The component of consciousness which is the experience in this tangled state is thus not sufficiently characterized.

It is questionable whether this malady can be overcome by inserting the distinction: 'which at first is excited through this'

This "at first" could not be temporal in nature, and so the specification would become ever more subtle.

(c) The delimitation would also have to be queried with regard to the phenomena of original association.

It is true that these phenomena would usually not be regarded as the primary, but only as secondary consequences of those stimulations which, coming from the peripheral nerve endings, excite a consciousness.

137|8   Yet certain abnormal cases give reason to believe ¦ that the opposite can also occur. There are cases of 'double consciousness': the lady continues with the sentence which she began months ago.

14. Just very briefly, let me point out that there is still something else in the definition which SULLY gives of experience (and the same holds for the one of LOTZE) which gives rise to misgivings.

Both are saying (as do many others) that an experience is a simple mental state. Indeed, this is the very basis of SULLY's claim that any another way of defining experience, such as an analytical one, is impossible. But it is very questionable, or, as we shall see, more precisely, it is really wrong that any experience could be called simple in the true and proper sense. Each one, rather, gives the opportunity to distinguish a multitude of parts. But this we will only demonstrate later. [. . .]

15. Another way of clarifying and delimiting the concept of experience is suggested by the physiologist PREYER.[40b#] Even though he does not pass off experience as something completely simple, but rather wants to see it as something 'as simple as possible', he nonetheless equally says: 'One cannot define what an experience is'. And then he adds: 'One can call it the content of a perception.[. . .] This expression is synonymous with the one of KANT that experience is the matter of perception or the matter of sensory knowledge'. Yet this harmony with KANT is of short duration, given that he continues to explain that experience does not correspond to the thing in itself, as KANT is meant to have claimed arbitrarily, rather experience is itself the thing in itself. Yet that [he says] is something for the metaphysician, not the psychologist.

Preyer: *Elemente der reinen Empfindungslehre*

16. We too do not wish to enter into the metaphysical question. But if we, as psychologists, examine the explanation we cannot possibly be satisfied with it.

'Content of perception' is meant to be equivalent to experience?

What sort of perceptions does he have in mind?

138|9   One speaks (and, in particular KANT spoke) of outer and : inner perceptions. Should all that which is the object of an outer or an inner perception be called experience? That would indeed be going much too far.

Experience and content of experience – everything would be confounded.

Or should we restrict the concept of perception to that which alone properly deserves the name, namely to the so-called inner perception?

In this case every judgment, desire, deciding, doubting, concluding or remembering would be an experience. Yet this is not only contrary to all linguistic usage but also to what is demanded by the discussion following the quotation in PEYER's treatise. For there, everything revolves around phenomena of colours, sound, etc., and their quality, their intensity and their combinations.

The determination must hence be regarded as totally inaccurate.

17. What other determination could more accurately be put forward in its place to characterize generally that [entity, i.e. experience,] the content of which we must now analyse?

I shall give one which I take to be flawless, even if it does have the inconvenience that its justification in one respect or another will only be given by later investigations: *An experience*, I say, *is a fundamental presentation of real physical phenomena (objects)* [*(Gegenstände)*].

18. The individual terms [used here] require a short explanation.

19. 'Physical phenomenon' (object) is opposed to psychical phenomenon.

20. 'Real' excludes all modifications, such as [the ones] brought about through negative [formulations, e.g.] through 'false', 'impossible', but also through 'past', 'future'. Consequently it also excludes the phenomena of original association.

148

21. 'Fundamental' [presentations] are opposed to superposed presentations, such as the so-called abstract presentations, something we shall have to discuss later.

22. All general presentations belong to the superposed ones. Every
|39|40 content of an experience is individual. |

23. All non-intuitive presentations belong also to the superposed ones.

24. And naturally also all contradictory ones.

There is never a contradiction or a conflict in the content of an experience.

To carry this discussion of the general character of experiences somewhat further let me add that the opposite is often claimed to be the case.

The followers of HERBART [claim that experience is a] thing with several properties (quality, intensity).

Physiologists [claim], for example, that the shore which apparently moves is in reality nonetheless stationary, and that in the railway the trees in the background appear to move forwards whereas actually they disappear towards the back.

My answer is that

(a) we are here not dealing with an experience, and that
(b) there is no contradiction in the phenomenon, but between two judgments, or between it and a judgment.

Another example put forward are ZÖLLER's lines before and after the crossing through [*Durchstreichung*] [with 'cross lines']; and yet no displacement has taken place, something which becomes clear by dimming the light [*Verdunkelung*] which makes the crosslines disappear. My answer here is again that

(a) we are not dealing with an experience, and that
(b) there is no contradiction in the phenomenon, but in the determination of measurement [*Massbestimmungen*] adopted by us. [. . .]

If the example is put forward that the same water feels warm to one hand and cold to the other, then I reply: the experience of temperature merely shows different temperature phenomena which,

149

spatially differing, bring out a contradiction in the way they present themselves. It is like black and white next to each other.

We may, however, be tempted to adopt contradictory assumptions. The claim, so often made by physiologists, that experience often contains contradiction is thus clearly only ¦ the consequence of their confounding what is not experience with what is.

140¦1

25. This sort of confusion often also appears in other contexts.

(a) Let me just briefly recall again the confusion arising through their speaking of experiences of pleasure and pain.
(b) Then I point at those cases where they talk of experiences of motion.
(c) Furthermore, I refer to the case where they speak of an experience of difference [*Unterschiedserfahrung*], like, for example, FECHNER's distinction between differences of experiences and experienced difference.[41] (In the latter case they enter consciousness as differences; in the former they exist between experiences but are not understood as differences.)

There can certainly be no objection to the division in itself, but there can well be one against the subsumption of the perception and the cognition [*Erkenntnis*] of a difference under experience.

What is to be thought of what has been experienced [*das Empfundene*] *qua* difference?

[Is it] the recognized fact that the one is not, and the other is?

In this case we have a negative judgment or an affirmative one with a negative predicate, neither given through experience.

Or, if we understand the matter differently:

There are certain positive determinations which exclude or are in conflict with one another, such that one can see from the partaking in one that it cannot partake in the other. Whatever partakes in the other cannot be identical with it, and thus must be different from it.

[We are dealing with a] *differentia* (*specifica*), it cannot be that the same surface can simultaneously be black and white and green and red in the same part.

These [positive determinations] are thus differences or contrasts. FECHNER uses the term 'contrast experience'. Whoever apprehends them somewhere as such, might it not be that he has [indeed] something which could be called 'experienced differences'? [The answer is that] he does not, if ¦ one remains true

141¦2

150

to the concept of experience. We are still dealing with a negative judgment, indeed a judgment which rejects [something] as impossible.

In consequence, the components [*Momente*] in question appear as being incompatible, as differences which characterize the one as being not identical with the other, [i.e. which] delimit [the one from the other]. HERTLING[42] [refers to the fact that] for every equality [there must be]

(1) one (at least individual) difference, [and]

(2) a component which is shared, an agreement in general.

The first one cannot be experienced because of the negation, the second one because of the generality.

Nota bene: Similar things (or [even] more) would have to be claimed if one were to speak of an experience of sameness.

(d) Yet another confusion, or confounding, is given if one speaks of a 'sense of space' [*Raumsinn*] which we are meant to have. It may in fact be in a certain sense correct that we have experiences of space [*Raumempfindungen*], indeed, it may even be correct that all experiences are experiences of space, insofar as every thing experienced appears as [spatially] located.

This experience of space is then at the same time an experience of quality, of colour, of warmth, etc. and maybe of many other things.

However, many people talk as if they had a peculiar class of experiences which are experiences of space and nothing else.

This is wrong.

One confuses a superposed presentation with a fundamental one, and a general one with an individual one. A space, apart from the qualitative differentiation, is something indeterminate, something general, something which is still capable of opposing differences. But it is impossible to present it intuitively to oneself without presenting filling qualities concomitantly.

Sometimes, a sense of space is thought to be still something different; it is seen as the freedom of the capacity to differentiate spatially. 'The sense of space of the tongue is finer than the one of the back' etc. ¦ 'The sense of space perfects itself through practice' etc.

142¦3

According to the earlier determination, it is clear that the use of this so-called sense has nothing to do with 'experiencing' in the proper sense.

(e) The expression sense of time [*Zeitsinn*] is equally confusing.

151

There cannot be an experience of time [*Zeitempfindung*].

The temporal, unlike the spatial, cannot even enter into determinations as an ingredient. (It is rather a matter of the original association; it is not 'real'.)

And it becomes even clearer that the activity of the so-called sense of time is not a matter of experiencing in the proper sense if one realizes that it is thought of as a capacity to correctly assess times.

(This is a fact; one also says for certain mentally ill people who cannot distinguish between what is long past and what has happened yesterday that they have lost the sense of time.)

It is an analogue to having a good eye [*Augenmass*] for assessing distances.

(f) It is obvious that in the case of expressions such as artistic sense, scientific sense, political sense, etc. we are not thinking of an experience in the described meaning. They are a pleasure [derived from] or talent for the correct judgment.

(g) Yet even if we hear someone talk of colour sense [sense of colour] we must not necessarily believe that we are always dealing with an experience in the true sense of the word.

What could be meant is a feeling for colouredness, for colour harmony. In other cases, however, the term will refer to the experience itself. This is so if I say of someone who is colourblind that he has an imperfect colour sense. It is meant to express that he is incapable of having certain experiences of colour which occur in other people.

However, in the case of the expression 'experience of colour' one has to be clear that it is similar to the one of 'experience of space'. In the same way in which one cannot have a pure experience of space, one cannot have a pure experience of colour. It would also be something indeterminate and general; whereas every experience shows something determinate and individualized [*Individualisiertes*]. In the same way in which the experience of space ¦ must simultaneously be qualitatively determined, the experience of quality must be spatially determined.

143¦4

26. Let me mention yet another case where experience is often confounded with something which is not experience.

One speaks of sensory deceptions. And many people presumably mean by this that it is the capacity of experience which here is subject to a deception. But this is impossible, because all deception, i.e. all error, finds itself in a judgment; yet experience is presentation!

It may deceive actively; but it cannot be subject to a deception.

Experience may be a presentation of something which does not actually exist. But this is not a deception.

An experience which is commonly used as a sign for something may at some time occur even though this some thing does not exist. But this is at most an active deception.

But often one is not clear about this. Signs for this are the pleonasm, the deception in judgment [*Urteilstäuschung*].

27. This should be sufficient to safeguard the use of the word experience and the word sense (which is so closely related to it) from the equivocations.

28. A special peculiarity of the contents of experience is involved in what we have set out here, a peculiarity which we now want to emphasize sharply and explicitly. We have said every content of experience is individual and determined. It possesses this determination through the fact that it is concrete in a peculiar way.

It grows out of a plurality of parts which we find in the same or in analogous manner in every content of an experiential presentation [*Empfindungsvorstellung*].

I have already touched upon these parts in what has been said earlier, but without reporting anything complete about them, something which we now wish to do.

And thus I say:

Every content of an experience shows itself as a concretum [composed of]:

(a) A peculiarity of place, a space [*Räumlichkeit*] of three dimen-
144|5   sions. ¦
(b) A quality which is not missing in any part of the space, even though it may vary in different places. In this regard one will have to investigate whether it itself is not a concretum composed of several parts, e.g.,
lightness (height);
quality in the more narrow sense;
furthermore one will have to investigate how the difference of saturation (rounding [*Rundung*]) and of lustre and gleam stand to this.

153

(c) A lightness (or, an analogue to it, such as the height of a tone) of which the same is true as has been said of quality.

(d) An intensity, which, multifariously varying, can also not be lacking in any part of the space of experience.

I shall now content myself with this without claiming that the 145|6 questions are exhaustively dealt with. |

Appendix 4

PSYCHOGNOSTIC SKETCH*

INTRODUCTION

1. Each one of us appears to himself in personal unity and particularity; what makes up this unity and particularity we refer to as our soul [*Seele*]. This soul shows itself in multifarious activity; it begins and ceases to be active in one way, while it remains constantly active in another way. As active, it is being affected, and, as active, it is effective, and hence it is [perceived as] substantial [*wesenhaft*]. In this regard, we speak of a plurality of activities of the soul. In being active, it has something as an object. DESCARTES referred to this having-as-an-object as thinking (in the most general sense). Others have called it consciousness (in the most general sense), or mentally having-present [*geistiges Gegenwärtig-Haben*], or mental holding [*geistiges Inhaben*], or intentional relation, or something else. Bearing in mind brevity and clarity, we shall call it having-an-object [*Gegenständlichhaben*], and the correlate being-an-object [*Gegenständlichsein*]. The specific relation of the soul, the soul-relation κατ' ἐξοχήν, consists in this.

2. From this is clear that our knowledge of the soul, of the activity of the soul, and of the relation of the soul belongs to the domain of a science. And one can thus well define psychology as the science of the soul, but equally well as the science of the activities of the soul, or as the science of the relations of the soul. It is most clearly defined as the science of the soul, its activities and its relations. The definition as the science of the relations of the soul has hardly ever been clearly put forward because they have not been sufficiently ¦

146¦7

* Outline of a psychognosy, begun on 4 September 1901 and finished on 7 September 1901. From the *Nachlass*. Registered as Ps 86.

155

divorced from the activities of the soul (denial of the generality of their existence; refutation). The definition as science of the soul has been branded in recent times to be 'metaphysical', which is meant to say as not justified by any experience, or even to be 'scholastic'. Yet with this, one has only expressed one's incompetence to do justice analytically to actual experience.

3. Psychology, in its nature, falls into two disciplines: psychognosy and genetic psychology.

4. Characteristics of psychognosy:

(a) profound differences to genetic psychology,
(b) psychognosy's relative independence, priority; almost purely psychological character of its statements; exactness.
(c) Independent value,
(d) difficulty: unnoticeability [*Unmerklichkeit*]; misinterpretability [*Missdeutlichkeit*]; restriction to one person; which is why it has only analogous validity for others; difficulty of measurement. How does one achieve completeness in it?

5. Methods of psychognosy:

(a) order,
(b) psychological microscopy,
(c) analogy,
(d) deductive replacement,
(e) genetic-psychological, physiological and physical auxiliary means;
(f) for the completeness of the survey [let me also say] this: *nihil est in intellectu, quod non prius fuerit in sensu*; entrance gates;
(g) count of the just-noticeable differences; interpretation of the WEBERian law.[42a] [. . .]

OF THE RELATIONS OF THE SOUL

1. They are divided according to the objects and according to the different ways of relating to the same object.

147|8 2. Of the different ways of relating: |

156

(a) The relations are multiplex [*vielheitlich*] or unified [*einheitlich*].

(b) The relations are explicit or implicit. [. . .]

(c) The relations are complex or simple. This is not to say that now they are one, and now they are several relations (this would provide no grounds for the formation of a class, or it would merely be subsumable under (a)). I have in mind here rather those cases where certain relations are inseparable from other relations; either mutually or one-sidedly. (Mutually such as: presenting of correlatives, evident accepting of correlatives, etc. One-sidedly such as: judging and presenting, to be pleased about something and to take it to be true; and again, within judging: predicating or denying and the simple accepting of the subject; as well as inferring and judging the premises; and within the realm of relating emotionally: desiring for the sake of some other and the desiring of this other.)

(d) The relations are relations of presenting, of judging and emotional ones, of which the last two give rise to distinctions regarding the different objects: the objects are partly phenomena, partly conceptual objects. (The question of conceptualism; refutation of nominalism.)

(e) They are furthermore partly physical, partly psychical.

(f) Finally, they are partly absolute, partly relative. They are multiple relations (of which one is inseparable from the other one) in being and thought and cognition.

3. The manner of presenting is not subject to any further divisions. Only a crossing with multiplex and unified; complex and simple; explicit and implicit is possible.

As an objection to this, it is put forward that presentations could be

(a) general and determined,

(b) clear and unclear,

(c) proper [*eigentlich*] and improper,

(d) intuitive and unintuitive; that they contain

(e) sensation and fantasy, as well as

148|9 (f) intensity. |

4. There are, in contrast, many divisions of the relations of judgment and the emotional relations.

157

5. Relations of judgment:

(a) affirmation and negation (claiming and denying);
(b) positing [*Setzen*] or simple denying and predicating or denying [*Absprechen*];
(c) immediate judging and inferring;
(d) unmotivated and motivated judging (to this belongs also what we recognize from concepts);
(e) apodeictic and assertoric judging;
(f) evident and blind judging;
(g) temporal differences. All judgments involve a temporal mode; in many of them it is a multiplex one, in which case they themselves are multiplex.

6. The differences of the degree of conviction are based on the differences of the objects. The question remains whether there are still other differences of intensity, and what they consist of.

7. The differences of the so-called quality are based on the differences of quality with indeterminate object.

8. The differences of the relation are based on the differences of the objects and on what we said about simplicity and complexity.

9. The differences of direct and indirect judgment are based on the differences of the objects: for example, God exists; it is true that God exists (= whoever judges that God exists, judges correctly).

10. The KANTian division into analytic and synthetic judgments is confused. Demonstration of its shortcomings.[43] What is, however, required is a tracing back to what is and is not evident from the concepts. Classes of judgments which are evident from concepts are:

(a) the denial of what is contradictory. In this lies the *principium indiscernibilium*. In this lies the principle of the excluded middle; [. . .]
(b) the denial of the union of positive opposites;
(c) the denial of the overdetermined;
(d) the denial of the undetermined;
(e) the denial that there is a judgment which in not affirming or negating; apodeictic or assertoric; ¦ past, present, or future;

149¦50

158

(f) the denial that what is good is bad, that what is true is false.

Comment: Contradictions: [the] positive exclusion of the third. A judgment is affirmative *or* negative. Emotional relations are love *or* hatred. Time is either the past or the present *or* the future. Judgments are apodeictic *or* assertoric. Magnitude is discretum *or* continuum.

11. Perceiving or apperceiving traces back to [the divisions into] implicit or explicit, multiplex or unified.

12. Distinguishing (mutually denying).

13. Judging disjunctively traces back to differences of the object. A or B is = one of A and B is.

14. Counting (see the earlier essay '*Von der Zahl*').[44]

15. *Emotional relations*: Apart from the differences arising through combining the division into presenting, judging and emotional relations with other ways of dividing (such as explicit and implicit etc. etc., see above – differences which are given through the difference of objects), emotional relations are already very diverse through the fact that, at one time, a pure presenting is given, at another time a presenting and a judging of the object which the emotional relation refers to, where the judgment is subject to multifarious specific differences [are given]. Thus, for example, in the case of simple love and joy or hope or longing or simple will.

16. However, in addition to this, there are still other exclusive specifications of emotional relations.

(a) Loving and hating is analogous to affirming or negating.
(b) Simple loving or simple hating and preferring or relegating [*Nachsetzen*]. (*Amor cui et cuius* and mere *amor cuius*.)
(c) To love for the sake of it – for the sake of some other (analogous to immediate judging and inferring).
(d) Motivated loving – unmotivated loving (analogous to motivated and unmotivated judging). Things are often also motivated through presenting, but not always. If I apperceive then there is no motivation through presenting, yet it is still a motivated judgment. I see the tree ¦ and apperceive my seeing; one then

150¦1

159

notices that the seeing causes the apperception in me, yet it is motivated through the existence of the other and not through the concept. If I love the means [*das Mittel*] motivatedly then it is not motivated through the concept but through the judgment.

(e) Characterized as being correct – or not characterized as being correct. (There is an analogy to that which in the cases of evidence is available from concepts; naturally it is not an analogue of seeing reason [*des Einsehens*], but an analogue of the being-recognizable-as-correct. Love which is characterized as being correct is recognizable as being correct. It is in this same way in which the [evident] judgment is recognizable as being correct). Is one, for instance, allowed to say that the analogue of 'a thing that is justifiably recognized as existing' [*des als seiend berechtigt erkennbaren Seins*] is 'a thing that is justifiably loved as being good' [*das als gut berechtigte Liebbarsein*]? This would lead to the possibility of it being recognized as something good, something that can be correctly loved.

Nota bene: 'Being justifiably lovable by being good' is then an analogue to 'being tenable as existing'.[45]

17. The will, in its particularity, is to be traced back to differences of the objects and to the judgment relations placed beside the emotional act. Willing always seems to be an indirect loving (loving as intending something to be realized through my acting).

18. Similar things are then true of choosing, where the incompatibility of a realization of a choice is shown by my loving characterized as being correct.

19. Remorse, intention – have a particular dependence on temporal differences in the underlying presenting and judging.

20. Intensity of emotional relations.

21. If one speaks of the content of a presentation, of a judgment or of an emotional relation, one is thinking of what is enclosed in it. Naturally, the whole of what is presented is enclosed in itself, in fact explicitly, but many other individually presented things are implicitly [enclose]. ([In] noticing of the tree [is] implicit the noticing of the leaves.) And the same [holds] for what is judged. Yet [enclosed] in it [i.e. in what is judged] is (apart from what other is implicitly

judged) also what is presented as such; which means that this, [too,] belongs to the content of the judgment. Furthermore, if an apodeictic judging takes place, then what is assertorically judged will also belong to the content of the judgment. And if an evident judging 151:2 takes place, then so will what is blindly judged (here, ¦ only a part of the content is dropped, namely the certainty). 'AB is not' belongs to the content of the negative judgment: 'A is not'. 'A is' belongs to the content of the affirmative judgment 'AB is'. The temporal component differentiates the content of the judgment; being motivated contributes to it. The predicating judgment seems to have the same (or equivalent?) content as a positing one, if one does not prefer to say that, in the case of the predicating judgment, two judgments have the same content as a positing judgment equivalent to them. (There is a red stone – a stone is red.) The question concerning the content of emotional relations is answered similarly.

22. Concerning the division of the *psychical [seelischen] relations according to the difference of their objects* we have already said that they fall into two classes:

(a) relations to phenomena,
(b) relations to conceptual objects.

23. It was further said that relations to phenomena divide into relations to

(a) physical phenomena, and

(b) psychical phenomena.

24. It is to be noted that physical and psychical phenomena can also confound themselves in *one* object.

25. Indeed, similar things must be admitted for phenomena and conceptual objects; in the case of an apperception, the object can be composed of phenomena and conceptual entities.

26. To complete the classification let me add that the relation to [physical] phenomena can also divide according to qualitative and spatial differences, and also that qualities are in part generic, in part

specific, while the spatial ones are only subject to a single differentiation. The qualitative differences are thus justifiably seen as the more noble ones and they are, above all, taken to be decisive in the classification.

27. Physical phenomena appear also as constant, or as changing with more or less speed. In their temporal determinations, they appear differentiated, though within very narrow boundaries, as present or
152¦3 as more or less past, ¦ which has to do with the fact that they all exist in us not only as presented, but also as psychically accepted [*anerkannt*]. Yet this is something which is equally valid for physical and psychical phenomena.

28. The sensory domains are divided according to the genera of physical phenomena [. . .].

29. Relations to *psychical* phenomena differ according to the differences of the psychical acts. We see [. . .] that they are partly sensory, partly supersensory. The sensory ones are partly perceptive ones, partly apperceptive ones. The perceptive ones are partly sensations in the narrower sense, partly affects. And then we see that the *supersensory* psychical acts are primarily directed partly upon intuitive objects, partly upon predicatively uniform [*einheitlich*] objects. Furthermore, that they are directed towards them partly as presenting, partly as judging, partly as emotional relations, whereas secondarily they show pure relations of thought. Accordingly, one could also divide them into pure activities of thought and emotional activities.

30. This then yields the full manifold of all psychical phenomena.
153¦4   [. . .] ¦

Appendix 5

PSYCHOGNOSTIC SKETCH: DIFFERENT ADAPTATION*

PSYCHOGNOSY

1. The human soul. [See the *Psychognostic Sketch*, Appendix 4].

2. The value of the science of the soul. Its domain is the whole of the inner world. From here one achieves the securing of the outer world. Logic, aesthetics, ethics, pedagogy, politics and practical dependence originate from here. The question of immortality, the comprehension of God in analogy to the soul, the concepts of cause and effect (ends and means) get their clarification here. We can only have immediate evident apperception of what is of psychical substance [*seelisch Wesenhaftem*] (and its insubstantial correlates). The assumption of an external world is initially hypothetical. The question is, in what sense knowledge of it is based on external experience, and in what sense it is rather based on internal experience.

3. The method.
   In general it is the method of natural science based on experience. But this is not saying much. Think of how different the methods of the different branches of natural science are! Each one must take into account the particularity and the particular difficulties of the subject.

4. What are the difficulties in this context?

(a) The difference of perception and apperception: what is inclusively apperceived [*einschliesslich Apperzipiertes*] is not really apperceived. What is perceived is, as such, not apperceived.

---

* From the Nachlass. Registered as Ps 86 (like Appendix 4).

163

The conditions of apperceiving are to be taken into account. What is always together cannot be apperceived separately. The localization of the senses is to be looked at. (Auditory feelings.) Animals do not apperceive in separation from what is strongly associated. One is to consider the non-apperceivability of smaller parts of the sensory field, [i.e. parts which are too small for a ! nerve excitation.

154!5

Bigger items too are still unnoticeably small. [We are dealing with] a comparative method to apperceive the characteristics. The impossibility of apperceiving the soul (that which differentiates what is mine from what is yours) constitutes a further difficulty. *Additional remark*: The difficulty of completeness: observance of the sources in perception, in experiencing and in noticing; unnoticed experiencing; unnoticed affect; unnoticed relations; characteristics (not unnoticed concept); non-apperceivability of the characteristics of the psychical act, of [the different] sides in the act itself; misinterpretability [*Missdeutlichkeit*].

(b) The limitation of the direct field of experience to one person; Daltonism[46] etc.; strengthening of the soul's state through scientific striving [*Forschungsstreben*]. The incompatibility [*Unverträglichkeit*] of anger etc. The consequence is a merely analogous validity of the knowledge of the soul (autognosy) for everyone else.

(c) Entanglement; dependence on physiological processes; physiology explains the most entangled natural phenomena; the backward state of brain physiology.

5. Methodical means:

(a) Order: From the more simple to the more complicated; separation of *psychognosy* and *genetic psychology*; the concept of the one [psychognosy] and the other [genetic psychology]; profound differences between the two; almost pure psychical character of the statements [of psychognosy]; near independence from physiology. [. . .] We are concerned here only with psychognosy. The task is big enough, and its value is not only to be seen in its being the foundation of the other, but also in itself. Let me furthermore point out the great practical importance of logic, ethics, and also the methodical rules specifically applicable to them, apart from the ones just mentioned.

(b) Psychological microscopy;

(c) analogy, for example lightness; good and true;

(d) looking back at what was earlier; frequent returning; greater clarity;

155¦6   (e) fixing the phenomenon through physiological means;¦

(f) analysis [*Erschliessen*] of the definitely unnoticed and unnoticeable;

Example: Analysis of tones, vowels, the soul; continuity of experience.

PSYCHOLOGY

1. Psychology is the science of the soul.

2. As such, its task is, above all, to analyse the phenomena of the soul in order to arrive at the parts which all phenomena of the human soul are composed of, and to determine each of these parts according to its manifold characteristics. Involved in this may also be the establishing of compatibility or incompatibility, and separability or inseparability of certain sub-phenomena. This part of psychology is called *psychognosy.*

Psychology, furthermore, has to explain the law according to which the phenomena of the soul come into being and cease to be. Further questions may be added here, such as whether the soul itself ceases to exist with the cessation of the phenomena of the soul, as well as the question concerning the beginning or the being without a beginning, the end or the indefinite continuation of the soul, and possibly the question concerning its manner of existing and its life activities after the dissolution of the body. This part of psychology is called *genetic psychology.*

3. Differences between the two.

One can recognize that there is a natural division between the two parts of psychology. The first one [i.e. psychognosy] is almost independent of the second one, whereas this one [i.e. genetic psychology] presupposes without exception the first part, or certain truths belonging to it. (Complete independence does not exist anywhere, not even for mathematics with respect to mechanics, nor for the latter with respect to optics.) [. . .] The application of certain means to arouse particular psychical phenomena which are to be observed is thus indispensable in the analysis. The statements of genetic psychology have a psycho-physical character; the statements

165

of psychognosy an almost purely psychical one. I say 'almost' because a physical component cannot be excluded; after all, we are dealing with the psychical phenomena of this life.

In the next world they may be considerably different. It can be said that the statements of genetic psychology are, without exception, inexact. They are only valid for the average of the cases. Some exception remains possible. The statements of psychognosy are valid without exception.

4. Is psychognosy the doctrine of the elements of the inner life?

This determination is only correct if we use certain terms loosely, i.e. in an improper sense. First of all, life is used here in the sense of: phenomena of the living soul. And then 'element' is not always to be understood as last, indivisible part. It may be possible that such a part can be found in every psychical phenomenon, but there are, in any case, others which can be divided *in infinitum*.

There is yet another reason why the term 'element' here appears to be used in an improper sense. For it is not possible to distinguish completely mutually separable parts in psychical composita. Rather, one part is completely separable, but the others are not at all separable from it. [It is] only the whole [which] can more or less (and, in the extreme case, completely) be reduced to the only separable part. (Compare this with a relativum, such as, for example, something which has the same colour as something else, and the coloured thing which is coloured in itself.) The parts, however, to which the analysis of the psychognost leads back, are in a certain sense outermost and first things, namely first in that they are indispensable for the description of the overall character of a domain of the soul. Thus one must, for example, distinguish the extension of the visual field from the soul *qua* that thing which is seeing [the seeing-thing] an object. But it is not necessary to distinguish furthermore every trillionth part of this seeing-thing, each directed to a trillionth part of this field. It is sufficient to go back to that [completely separable] part; it, however, is indispensable.

5. The value of psychognosy

(a) in itself;
(b) for genetic psychology;
(c) for metaphysics (theology and cosmology);
(d) for ethics;

166

(e) for the whole of theoretical and practical philosophy;
(f) DESCARTES' and LEIBNIZ's *characteristica universalis.*

6. Psychognosy as an experiential science [*Erfahrungswissenschaft*].

There are sciences which, at least according to the *sententia communis*, are built up completely *a priori.* Psychognosy, in any case, is incapable of being so. It, too, must start with what is immediately evident. But [what, in its case, is immediately evident] are immediately evident facts which are not of apodeictic but of purely assertoric character. It is the sort of fact upon which every experiential science is based in its own way. Because each one must start with facts which are immediately evident. Yet this kind of fact we only possess in the perception of our psychical states, i.e. in the knowledge of that which appears to us as *psychical.* It is true that we are inclined by nature also to accept other facts as immediately evident. In the same way in which someone immediately accepts himself as the one who is seeing [as seeing-thing], he will always also immediately accept something which is seen [a seen-thing], and, in fact, he will not only immediately accept it as something which is being seen by him (for as such it is a necessary correlate to himself as the one who is seeing), but also he will immediately accept it as something real [a real-thing], for example, as a spatially extended red[-thing]. But in doing this, he judges blindly. The existence of this real red[-thing] is not immediately evident, what is immediately evident, rather, is the existence of himself as someone who is seeing this red[-thing] and the existence of this red[-thing] as something seen by him. (Considering [the matter] more closely, the scientist will thus condemn this blind judgment by means of an evident judgment, as being logically inadmissible, yet without removing it for this reason.) Such a pair of correlates is given to us in every immediately evident experience, a pair the first half of which is an intrinsic [*wesenhaftes*], and the other half a non-intrinsic something. The intrinsic one is our soul *qua* being put in relation; the non-intrinsic one its correlate, i.e. something which our psychical activity is directed at, *qua* being so.

7. The multipart nature of psychical phenomena and the multiplicity of their correlates.

Everything psychical which we apperceive is composed. It is an accident which includes the substance of the soul, or a plurality of accidents of the same substance, each of which contains this substance. Each phenomenon of the soul has several correlates, a primary object and a secondary one, the latter being the phenomenon itself, given as an object.

8. Classification of the psychical phenomena from a psychognostic viewpoint.

Psychical phenomena can be divided into massive [i.e. composed] ones and ultimate unified ones [*letzteinheitliche*]. The former are also called sensitive and the latter intellective ones. Psychical phenomena can furthermore be divided into presenting ones, judging ones and emotional ones, according to the way they are related to the primary object. Strictly speaking, all psychical phenomena are massive because of the continuity which they have as temporally apparent things [*Zeitlicherscheinende*]. But apart from this continuity, conceptually thinking-things, as such, do not have any continuity, but seeing-things and hearing-things etc., as such, do. With regard to the secondary object, all psychical phenomena are judging or emotional in a way which immanently includes the one of judging.

9. Classification of sensitive phenomena into sensations and affects.

Sensitive phenomena are either sensations or affects. In the case of the former, the primary and the secondary object are accepted blindly (and thus presented immanently); in the latter case, both are emotionally apprehended in a way not characterized as not being correct (and thus immanently blindly accepted and immanently presented). The fact that all sensitive objects appear as accepted (really or immanently) gives them the character of what appears as existing. The fact that all objects of affect appear emotionally apprehended gives them the character of something pleasant or unpleasant.

10. Classification of sensations.

All sensations display spatially qualitative features. As being spatial, the objects display differences running into infinity which, however, are all coordinated. As being qualitative, they show themselves either different in genus, like what is coloured [colour-things] and what sounds [tone-things], or merely different in species like what is red [red-things] and what is blue [blue-things]. The groups of sensations of the senses are divided according to the genera of quality.

11. Common peculiarities of the groups of sensations of the senses.

159|60   The primary object of every sensory phenomenon, ¦ whatever sense it belongs to, is always spatially extended. If, in its extension, it has unnoticeably small gaps, then it appears diluted. We speak of diminished intensity. Unbrokenness [*Lückenlosigkeit*] is the maximum of intensity. In the same way in which there can be unnoticeably small absolute gaps, there can be unnoticeably small relative gaps, such as, for example, in the change from blue to red in unnoticeably small parts; we then speak of mixed qualities. Furthermore, there is a contrast between light and dark for colours as there is between high and deep for tones. The one is analogous to the other, and such an analogue exists for every sensory domain. When I said there is a contrast between light and dark, I was not precise. This contrast actually only exists between black and white as the extreme of dark and the extreme of light. Everything else is after all to a lesser degree light as well as dark. Grey appears in this as a mixture of black and white, and it is lighter or darker grey according to the ratio of both. For a fully saturated colour, for example pure red, there is a distance from black and a distance from white, and there is a ratio between the two distances. If, for example, it is 3:2, then pure red will be of the same lightness as a grey in which black and white are mixed as 3:2. All pure red has this level of lightness. If we speak of light red or dark red, we can explain this through the mixing in of other colours (saturated or unsaturated). In analogy to this we are to think of an absolute tone lightness and tone darkness. The former is approached by the highest tones of the scale, the latter by the deepest ones, and they obviously differ from the tones situated in the middle through a lesser saturation. They [these highest and deepest tones, respectively] always get closer to one another, which indicates that the tones at different levels of height differ, like light red from dark red, through the mixing in of other tones, in particular absolute tone lightness (tone white, so to speak) and absolute tone darkness (tone black, so to speak). Between qualities of the same sense there

160|1   can be (as demonstrated by the tone sense) such a ¦ gradual transition from simple to even simpler qualities that the transition appears to us like something continuous, in that the jumps are unnoticeable. Should this [in individual cases] not equally be the case for the visual sense, then this is to be put down to a less perfect development [of this sense]. We are all blind to so many colours that the distances between given pure colours are very noticeable. The distance in lightness from pure saturated tones is zero or very small compared

169

to their distance in lightness to the pure tone white or tone black. The distance in lightness of pure saturated colours ought also to be zero, or it is in any case very small compared with the distance of each of them from black, on the one hand, and from white on the

161:2   other. [. . .] :

Appendix 6

PERCEIVING, APPERCEIVING CLEARLY APPERCEIVING, COMPOUNDED APPERCEIVING TRANSCENDENTALLY APPERCEIVING*47

1. Wherever something is presented, one apperceives. There is no perceiving without some apperception.

2. If a whole is apperceived, then it is not always the case that each part is apperceived in particular. Yet it will nonetheless be included in the apperceived object. One says that it is perceived without being apperceived.

3. Sometimes not only the whole but also a part is apperceived in a particular apperception. The one as well as the other object will then be apprehended, but the one will not be apprehended as [being] part of the other.

4. Yet it also sometimes happens [that the one is actually apprehended as being part of the other]. We then say that the whole is not only apperceived as a whole but also as containing the part, or, that the whole is clearly apperceived as containing this part [*diesem Teile nach deutlich apperzipiert*].

5. And thus, the whole can be apperceived as containing many other parts, indeed it can be apperceived as containing a multiplicity of parts which together equal the whole. Yet it will still remain apperceived with poor clarity if there remain apperceived parts containing parts which are merely perceived, or which, although being apperceived, are not apperceived as parts of the parts.

* From the Nachlass. Registered as Ps 29.

6. Similar to the way in which the continuum can be clarified through apperception of particular parts of a continuum as parts thereof, it is also possible to clarify a logical whole through apperception of particular parts of this whole as parts.

7. Again, this case must be distinguished from the one where the part concerned, as well as the logical whole, is apperceived, but not as a logical part of this whole.

162¦3

8. In this case, however, the logical part has the peculiarity that it remains recognizable, if not as part of this whole, then all the same as part of some logical whole. Thus the immediate insight that, for example, there cannot be any colour which would not be further differentiated in some way.

9. Now, amongst these logical parts are also the relative and collective determinations in general. In the same way in which we can apprehend a red-thing [*ein Rotes*], a redder- than-a-less-red-thing [*ein Röteres als ein minder Rotes*], and a partly-redder-and-partly-less-red-thing [*ein zum Teil Röteres, zum Teil minder Rotes*].

10. The logical parts of the relativa and the collectiva can be more general or less general. Two things of the same red, or two things of the same magnitude are both less general than two things which are the same in some [indefinite] respect.

11. It appears that ARISTOTLE was of the opinion that such a far-reaching abstraction cannot be carried out. And that it is not synonymy but rather analogy which is given in this use of the term 'same'.

12. But what does analogy mean? ARISTOTLE himself gives the answer: the sameness of proportions which exist in the one and the other genus. But surely this is talking of sameness in a uniform [*einheitlichem*] sense. If I say that what is affirmative [an affirmative-thing] is to what is negative [a negative-thing] as what is loving [a loving-thing] to what is hating [a hating-thing], I characterize what is loving as standing to what is hating in the same way as what is affirmative stands to what is negative, i.e. I characterize the one as being roughly the same as the other and *vice versa*.

13. And thus it seems that the abstraction of a uniform concept 'same', transcendent for each of these genera, becomes possible. The same concept will also be applicable for many other genera given to us.

14. And the same is then true of many other relative concepts, such as that of part and whole.

15. An interesting question is whether this is also true of the so-called psychical relations, even though they are not proper relations. If this is the case, then they can also be applied synonymously to bodies and to God. It is presumably more correct that such abstractions are, at least for us, impossible, and that we can thus attribute only analoga
|63|4   to, say, bodies. And likewise to God. |
It is thus possibly also more correct to say that such bodies (and topoids of n dimensions) and also God are to be characterized not as being 'personal' [in the sense of being a person] but rather as being 'analogous to what is personal'.

EDITORS' NOTES

To keep a correspondence to the numbering of the notes in the original German edition, the notes which are new in this edition are numbered by adding alphabetic indices.

1 Brentano criticizes the 'imperfection of the present methods of investigation' and demands that we see the 'unity of the species' (a term which has 'the same sense in every context') both in the domain of colours and in the one of sounds. In the case of colours, as in the one of sounds, we are given: 'the contrast between clear and dark'; or 'high and low'; 'saturation and non-saturation'; 'mixtures'; 'maybe levels of mixture'; 'maybe equal specific brightness'; 'intensity'; [*Psychognostische Skizze* (1901), from Ps 86, pp. 14–16].

2 Johannes Müller, *Handbuch der Physiologie des Menschen*, 2 vols., 1833/40.

3 H. Helmholtz [German physicist and physiologist, 1821–1894], *Die Lehre von den Tonempfindungen als physiologische Grundklasse für die Theorie der Musik*, 4th ed., Braunschweig: Vieweg, 1877, pp. 113–193.

4 In connection with vowels, Brentano speaks of the 'blending' [*Verschmelzung*], involved in the hearing of such sounds, as in the hearing of an umlaut like ä and ö: '. . . in this case the blending is so deep that many do not even suspect it to be a multitude of overtones.' [*Untersuchungen zur Sinnespsychologie*, 2nd ed., Hamburg: Meiner, 1979, pp. 218 f.]

4ª C.F. Zöllner, German physicist, 1834–1887.

5 See D. Hume, *A Treatise of Human Nature*, Book 1, Part IV, Section vi ('Of Personal Identity').

6 Brentano was later to reject the 'modification theory' of proteraesthesis. The past experiences that are involved in proteraesthesis are *entia*

175

irrealia. And yet they form a continuum bounded by *entia realia* – by actual things that have no such modifying attributes. But how can things so heterogeneous as *entia realia* and *entia irrealia* form a continuum in which 'what is non-real would be less different from what is real than what is non-real from what is non-real; indeed infinitely different from it?' [Brentano writing to Marty, 1894, quoted in Kraus: '*Zur Phäno-menognosie des Zeitbewusstseins'. Archiv für die gesamte Psychologie* 75 (1930), pp. 1–22, the quotation appears on p. 7]. Colours and sounds cannot form a continuum, for they are of different species. How, then, can things/what is real and non-things/what is non-real form a continuum?

Indeed, the 'modification theory' really leaves us with our problem, as Brentano came to see. Sentences containing such modifying ex-pressions as 'supposed king' and 'false gold' can be rephrased in sentences that do not contain such expressions. Thus, 'He is a supposed king' tells us that the person in question is thought to be a king, and 'That is false gold' tells us that the thing in question, though it may be thought to be gold, is not in fact gold. If 'past' and 'future' are thought to be modifying expressions, then, Brentano suggests, we should try to make a similar paraphrase of the sentences in which they appear. We will find we cannot succeed. See Brentano's letter to Marty, of March 1906, reprinted in Brentano's *Die Abkehr vom Nichtrealen*, Hamburg: Meiner 1966, pp. 160–5.

We consider, then, this possibility: temporal differences within experience are to be thought of, not as differences in the objects that we are conscious of, but as differences in the ways in which we are conscious of the objects. (This move will call to mind Kant's 'Coper-nican Revolution' and the doctrine that time is a 'form of inner sense'. But Brentano's view can hardly be called Kantian. This latter point is obvious in view of Brentano's doctrine according to which what is real coincides precisely with what is temporal or 'in time'.) It is presupposed, then, that there are *temporal modes* of consciousness. Brentano first thought that such temporal modes apply primarily to judgment. It is one thing to affirm an object as now (i.e. to affirm the object *simpliciter*); it is another thing to affirm the object as past; and it is still another to affirm the object as future.

But Brentano did not hold that there are only three modes of temporal judgment. He held, rather, that there can be a continuum of temporal judgments. This continuum is crudely illustrated in the judgment of something being 'more and more past'. But judgment is not the only intentional attitude that may be directed toward the past and the future. What we call past things and future things may also be emotional objects – objects of love or hate – without thereby being judged. And they may be simply objects of thought, without thereby being loved or hated, accepted or rejected. This leads Brentano to his final view. The fact that there are temporal differences within experience is a function, not merely of different temporal modes of *judgment* but of temporal modes of presentation [*Vorstellung*]. It is one thing for a note, say, to be presented as present and another thing for it to be presented as past. The judgments

176

we make are a function of the presentations that underlie them and we would not be able to make judgments about the past or about the future unless we had these temporal modes of presentation. And the same holds for the emotions.

The proper description of proteraesthesis, then, is this: 'In that what was initially given as present is appearing more and more as past, it is not that we accept that there exist *other objects*, but we accept *the same object* in a different way, in a different mode of accepting'. (*Philosophische Untersuchungen zu Raum, Zeit, und Kontinuum*, Hamburg: Meiner 1976, p. 96; compare *Vom sinnlichen und noetischen Bewusstsein*, Hamburg: Meiner, 1974, pp. 45–52.) The temporal modes of judgment are a function of the temporal modes of presentation. One judges in a temporal mode if one accepts what is presented in that temporal mode.

7 The apodeictic judgment 'There is a truth' would be an affirmative apodeictic judgment. But according to Brentano's later view, the only apodeictic judgments we make are negative. Brentano sometimes says that apodeictic judgments are those judgments 'which either accept something as *necessary* or reject something as *impossible*'. However, he does not define apodeictic judgments by reference to necessity and impossibility. Rather, he defines necessity and impossibility by reference to the concept of an apodeictic judgment.

An apodeictic judgment, according to Brentano, is a judgment which is motivated. 'A judgment is motivated [*motiviert*] if it is directly caused by another mental phenomenon, and if we perceive this causation. In the case of apodeictic judgments we have a motivation by the matter of presentation [*Vorstellungsmaterie*]. One speaks of assertorial judgments, if this kind of motivation is not present. Assertorial hence indicates a mere privation, the motivation by the matter of presentation is not given.' (*Die Lehre vom richtigen Urteil*, Hamburg: Meiner 1956, pp. 128 f.)

In the typical case of an apodeictic judgment, one considers a certain compound content – say a thing that is both round and square. The thinking of this content directly causes one to reject it: one perceives that the thinking of this content is the cause of the rejection of it. And the rejection is directly evident. (See *Die Lehre vom richtigen Urteil*, p. 168.) One is then said to reject the round square apodeictically, and one may express this apodeictic rejection by saying 'Round squares are impossible'. Thus Brentano says that 'where there is apodeictic evidence [*Evidenz*], there is always an evident perception of the causality, and hence a multiple evident perception'. [*Die Abkehr vom Nichtrealen*, pp. 219 f.]

If the thought content should directly cause one to accept the content, and if one were to perceive this causation, then the apodeictic judgment would be affirmative and one could express oneself by saying that the object thought of is necessary. But we do not in fact make such affirmative apodeictic judgments, according to Brentano's later view, even though such affirmative apodeictic judgments *could* be made.

Judgments of *possibility* are also apodeictic judgments. In judging that

177

A is possible, we apodeictically reject statements which (correctly) reject A [we apodeictically reject correct rejectors of A]. Thus Brentano does not recognize Kant's category of problematic judgments. For the latter category, according to Kant, is not apodeictic and yet comprises judgments of possibility and impossibility.

Some of Brentano's observations suggest that his theory of the modal judgment may be called an expressive theory, for it is similar to the expressive theories of ethical judgments that were defended by many philosophers in the middle of the present century. An expressive theory of ethics tells us that sentences ostensibly predicating an ethical characteristic of something (e.g. 'Pleasure is intrinsically good', 'Stealing is wrong') *express* certain states of mind, but do not actually assert anything about the world. Those who held the emotive theory of ethics held that the states of mind expressed by ethical statements are neither true nor false – neither correct nor incorrect. But Brentano holds that the apodeictic judgments expressed by modal statements are either correct or incorrect. The statements expressing such judgments may be true or false. Our apodeictic judgments are all negative; they are all rejections.

But when Brentano discusses St Anselm's ontological argument and the idea of God, he suggests that, if we *could* have an adequate or complete idea of God, then the having of such an idea would cause an apodeictic acceptance. 'For us it is sufficient to realize here that "God exists" would actually be a truth which in itself would be immediately evident for the one who possessed the adequate idea [*Vorstellung*] of God.' [*Vom Dasein Gottes*, Hamburg: Meiner 1968, p. 58.] But evidently this would be the only possible occasion for a correct affirmative apodeictic judgment. (See Kastil's footnote 11 on p. 533 of *Vom Dasein Gottes*).

Brentano's proofs that there is a necessary being do not yield necessary propositions as their conclusions. Each proof is a *reductio ad absurdum*: one premise says that there are contingent things; another says that if there were no necessary being then there would be no contingent things; and the assertorial conclusion is that there is a necessary being.

8 'In accepting [*anerkennen*], e.g. a sparrow, I also accept a bird, because bird is a *logical* part of the sparrow, and I accept a beak, because it is a *physical* part of the sparrow' [*Wahrheit und Evidenz*, Hamburg: Meiner 1974, p. 99]. Thus thinking [*Denken*] is a logical part of experiencing [*Empfinden*]; experiencing is a logical part of seeing [*Sehen*]; seeing is a logical part of seeing-red [*Rotsehen*]. In his *Würzburger Kolleg* on metaphysics, Brentano said this about logical parts: 'The logical whole is an individual of a genus. A logical part is each part of its definition, i.e. genus, difference, further difference (difference of difference) and so forth down to the lowest generality'. It is typical of logical parts 'that the distinctional separability is only one-sided.' (The unpublished *Würzburger Metaphysikkolleg* is in the Brentano-*Nachlass* at Brown University, Providence, RI, USA, under the reg. no. M 96 I and II.)

Can the concept of parts which are (mutually) pervading [*durch-wohnend*] be reduced to that of logical parts? If we speak of the spatiality [*Räumlichkeit*] or the quality of a sensation, we are not speaking of the subspecies of the sensation or the genus under which it falls. The concept of logical parts is illustrated in a different way in sensation. For example, seeing-red has seeing as a logical part; seeing has experiencing as a logical part, and experiencing has thinking as a logical part. Analogously, judging is a logical part of accepting. But the affirmative quality would be a pervading part of accepting. 'Logical parts' would seem appropriate for species and genera, not for individual things; and 'mutually pervading parts' would seem appropriate for individual things and not for species and genera.

8[a] In this paragraph, Brentano summarizes very succinctly his fundamental doctrine of intentionality. Every 'psychical phenomenon' – by which I mean Brentano's 'actually separable parts of consciousness' – displays, as defining characteristic, a certain relational structure, namely that of an 'intentional' or 'primary psychical' relation. Like every relational structure, a psychical phenomenon is thus meant to show two correlates: an act of *consciousness*, say A (which Brentano refers to as the 'subject' of the intentional relation), and that which A is 'directed upon', say C (the 'object' of the relation). But what is this second correlate? In the examples put forward by Brentano in this paragraph, we find, for example, that the second correlate to the act of seeing [*Sehen*], say A_S, given in a visual experience S is described as 'what is seen' [*das Gesehene*], say C_S. At first, it might thus seem that C_S is taken to be the real object (say, the chair in front of the person who is seeing). But this is clearly *not* what Brentano had in mind, for he tells us that the defining characteristics of intentional pairs of correlates (and hence implicitly of psychical phenomena) is that *only* the first correlates, i.e. the acts of consciousness, are real, and never the second ones. This obviously excludes the chair in front of the seeing person from being the second correlate, or 'immanent object', of his act of seeing.

The correct interpretation, in my view, can be derived from the fact that Brentano sometimes paraphrases 'direction upon an object' by 'reference to a content': I take it that the second correlate C_S is meant to be the *content* of A_S. Thus when Brentano uses the (admittedly somewhat opaque) phrase 'the person being thought' [*der gedachte Mensch*] to talk about the second correlate to an act A_T of thinking, he is not talking about a peculiar kind of people, but about the content of A_T. His use of the terms 'thinking' and 'person' in this context is merely to indicate that the content in question (C_T) is a content of a *thought* about a *person*. Similarly, we are to interpret his use of 'the thinking of the person' [*das Denken des Menschen*] in referring to A_T as indicating that this act of consciousness is not merely an act of *thinking*, but indeed an act of thinking about a person.

If this interpretation of Brentano's views is correct, then psychical phenomena – be they phenomena of thinking ('thoughts'), or seeing,

179

or whatever – all possess a particular asymmetrical relational structure, symbolically representable as A→C, with (a) a particular act A of consciousness – e.g. of thinking, seeing, etc. – and (b) the content C of this act, as correlates. Indeed, Brentano saw this as the defining characteristics of what is psychical. It must also be emphasized that Brentano saw these correlates occurring as parts of psychical phenomena as merely distinctionally separable from one another. It is thus imposs-ible to have an act of consciousness without a correlated content and *vice versa*. Psychical phenomena (the actually separable parts of consciousness) are thus neither merely acts nor merely contents, but wholes in which content and act are inseparably related through intentionality. This must be kept in mind even when Brentano himself chooses to refer to these phenomena merely as 'psychical acts' (cf. p. 87). For an additional explication of these notions see, for example, B. Smith, 'The Soul and Its Parts II: Varieties of Inexistence', in *Brentano Studien* IV, Brentano Forschung: Würzburg 1993.

9 Brentano is evidently referring to *Metaphysics*, 1021a, 30.

10 ''Ἐπεὶ δ' αἰσθανόμεθα ὅτι ὁρῶμεν καὶ ἀκούομεν [. . .]' ('Since it is through sense that we are aware that we are seeing or hearing [. . .]'). Aristotle, *De Anima*, Book III, Chapter 2, 425b, 12: transl. by J.A. Smith].

11 What does Brentano mean when he says that every psychical act has itself as a secondary object? Brentano had discussed the question in detail in the first edition of the *Psychology from an Empirical Standpoint* (Book II, Chapter 3), but there remain certain difficulties in interpreting the doctrine. The most plausible interpretation may seem to be: every psychical act is such that, when it occurs, then it is evident to the subject that the act occurs. But Brentano also says that nothing is evident to a subject unless the subject *judges* that thing with evidence. Thus, he says in the present lectures that evidence is 'not to be found anywhere outside the judgment'. Brentano would not affirm that every psychical act is accompanied by an evident judgment to the effect that this act occurs. For, since the evident judgment would itself be a psychical act, the view would involve an infinite regress. And Brentano denies that there is such a regress, saying that the series stops with its first member.

Moreover, Brentano usually formulates the doctrine of secondary consciousness, not with reference to evidence, but by means of such sentences as the following: 'In the presenting [*das Vorstellen*] of the colour is simultaneously a presenting of this presenting'. 'The ex-periencing of the colour and the concomitant experiencing of this experiencing are directed towards different objects' (p. 27 of this volume). Yet these words, too, suggest the danger of a regress. But Brentano does not mean to say that every presenting [*Vorstellen*] is the object of *another* presenting, or that every experiencing is the object of *another* experienicng. So in what sense can these acts be said to have themselves as primary objects?

Brentano does *not* mean to say that every psychical act is the primary object of an evident judgment. In what sense, then, can every psychical act be said to be evident to the subject – if evidence can nowhere be found in experience?

The answer – which Brentano never makes explicit – would seem to be this. The occurrence of the psychical act may be said to be evident to the subject in the following *extended* sense: every psychical act is necessarily such that, if one perfoms that act and at the same time judges that one performs it, then one judges with evidence that one performs it.

To say, then, that the experiencing of a colour is always accompanied by the concomitant experiencing of this experiencing is to say this: the experiencing of the colour is necessarily such that, if someone experiences in this manner and at the same time judges that he does so, then he judges with evidence.

In this sense, then, Brentano can say that 'everything psychical falls under inner perception' (pp. 129 of the present volume). Everything psychical is necessarily such that, if it occurs, and if at the same time one judges that it occurs, then one judges with evidence. And if Brentano adds, 'but this does not mean that everything is noticed', he reminds us, that something psychical can occur, without our judging that it does occur.

It should be noted that he identifies 'consciousness in the narrower sense' with noticing (Appendix 5). Hence it is only in an extended sense of consciousness that every psychical act can be said to be an object of consciousness. Compare Brentano's discussion of these questions in 'On Mental Reference to Something as a Secondary Object' in *Psychology from an Empirical Standpoint*, pp. 275–8.

12 See *De Anima*, Book III, Chapter 2, 425b, 22: Ἔτι δὲ καὶ τὸ ὁρῶν ἔστιν ὡς κεχρωμάτισται. τὸ γὰρ αἰσθητήριον δεκτικὸν τοῦ αἰσθητοῦ ἄνευ τῆς ὕλης ἕκαστον. ('Further, in a sense even that which sees is coloured; for in each case the sense organ is capable of receiving the sensible object without its matter'.)

The problem here seems to be this: if a person who is seeing-red [*ein Rotsehender*] were *ipso facto* red, then red would be the specific difference that marks off seeing-red [*Rotsehen*] from seeing, and seeing would be the specific difference that marks off seeing-red from red. But one of these things must be false.

13 Laura Bridgman (1829–1889) lost both her sight and her hearing as a result of an attack of scarlet fever when she was two years old. The systematic education she received at the Perkins Institute for the Blind, in Boston, attracted the attention of many nineteenth-century psychologists.

14 According to Brentano's earlier conception, judgments may be divided into those which accept a certain content and those which simply reject or deny a certain content. But, according to his later theory of judgment,

acceptance may be accompanied by one or the other of two additional attitudes – one of them affirming something further of the content accepted and the other denying something of the content accepted. The two expressions 'to accept' ['*anerkennen*'] and 'to reject' ['*verwerfen*'] are to be supplemented by the two further expressions, 'to attribute' (or 'to grant') ['*zusprechen*'] and 'to deny' ['*absprechen*']. '*Zusprechen*' may be rendered somewhat roughly as 'to predicate something of something', and '*absprechen*' as 'to deny something of something'. These locutions express what Brentano called 'double judgments' ['*Doppelurteile*']. These are judgments 'which accept something and attribute to it or deny it other things'. Compare the footnote on p. 194 of *Psychologie vom empirischen Standpunkt* (not contained in the English translation). I make a double judgment when (a) I make a simple ('thetic') affirmative judgment which I can express in the form, 'There is an S', and (b) I then supplement this affirmation either by a further attributing [*Zuerkennen*] ('and what is more it is a P') or by a denying [*Absprechen*] ('and what is more it is not a P'). If an I-judgment ('Some S is P') is interpreted as a double judgment, then the judger has (a) accepted an S and (b) has predicated P of S. And if an O-judgment ('Some S is not P') is interpreted as a double judgment, then the judger has (a) accepted an S and (b) has denied P of S. The O-judgment, according to this conception, is an affirmative judgment, since it is a matter of accepting an S. Yet Brentano concedes, it is partly negative in that it is 'a kind of denying in which that, of which something is denied, is accepted'. [*Psychologie vom empirischen Standpunkt*, Vol. III, p. 9; English tr.: *Sensory and Noetic Consciousness*, L.L. McAlister and M. Schättle, London: Routledge 1981.] The I-judgment, on this interpretation, does coincide with what Aristotle had called combinings or judgments of synthesis. And the O-judgments would seem to coincide with what he called the *diaeresis* of subject and predicate.

Brentano seems to have had two different psychological interpretations of the 'synthesis' that takes place in the case of an I–judgment. According to the one, the synthesis does express a two-fold judgment – first, a simple accepting and then an attributing or a denying. According to the other interpretation, the synthesis takes place wholly within the sphere of ideas [*Vorstellungen*] and the judgment is simply an affirmation of the result. [See Anton Marty, *Untersuchungen zur Grundlegung der allgemeinen Grammatik und Sprachphilosophie*, Halle: Niemeyer 1918, pp. 341 ff. and his *Gesammelte Schriften*, Vol. II, Part 1, Halle: Niemeyer 1918. See also Kastil's notes to the *Kategorienlehre*, Hamburg: Meiner 1974, p. 371.]

14ᵃ I take it that *Ideenflucht* is the same as that accelerated and digressing train of thought symptomatic of pathological mania which in English clinical terminology is referred to as 'flight of ideas'.

14ᵇ F.A. Trendelenburg, German philosopher 1802–1872, Brentano's teacher in Berlin. For Zeno-type arguments in Hegel and his followers, see F.A. Trendelenburg, *Die logische Frage in Hegels System*, Leipzig: Brockhaus 1843, esp. p. 27.

15 Compare, in this context, Brentano's tenth habilitation postulate, reprinted in *Über die Zukunft der Philosophie*, 2nd ed., Hamburg: Meiner 1968, pp. 138–9; F. Brentano, *Geschichte der griechischen Philosophie*, Bern: Francke 1963, pp. 134–8. Concerning Hegel's treatment of the paralogism, see the jubilee edition of H. Glockner, Vol. 19, Stuttgart-Bad Cannstatt: Frommann 1965, pp. 577–9. In the same context, see also the exposition and critique of Hegel's theory of inference by Trendelenburg in *Logische Untersuchungen*, Leipzig: Hirzel 1962, pp. 326–59. As concerns the key word paralogism, see also Trendelenburg's *Erläuterungen zu den Elementen der aristotelischen Logik*, Berlin: Bethge 1842, pp. 67–9.

16 Th. Gomperz, Austrian philologist and philosopher, 1832–1912, friend and colleague of Brentano. Gomperz objects to Brentano's interpretation of Aristotle, i.e. to the maintained unity of the *corpus Aristotelicum* (see Th. Gomperz, *Griechische Denker* III, Berlin/Leipzig: De Gruyter 1931, pp. 179 f.), and is answered by Brentano in *Aristoteles Lehre vom Ursprung des menschlichen Geistes*, Hamburg: Meiner 1980, p. 28.

17 Brentano here refers to his analysis of the traditional A-, E-, I- and O-judgments. Compare *Psychology from an Empirical Standpoint*, pp. 205–20.

The simplest of these is the *I-judgment* ('He judges that some S are P'). Like simple thetic affirmation, it is an acceptance, but unlike simple thetic affirmation, it involves a compound of two terms. We may treat the I-judgment either as a complex thetic judgment or as a double judgment. In the first case, it could be put as 'He accepts an S which is a P'. The expression 'S which is P' and 'P which is S' are mutually exchangeable; hence Brentano says there is no significant distinction between the subjects and the predicates of such judgments. In the second case, the I-judgments would become: 'He accepts an S and predicates a P of it'.

The *O-judgment* ('He judges that some S are not P') is a double judgment involving a denial [*ein Absprechen*] We may put it as 'He is an acceptor of one who correctly denies P of an S.' If negative terms are admitted, then the O-judgment may be construed, not as a double judgment, but as a thetic acceptance: 'He accepts an S which is a non-P'.

The *E-judgment* ('He judges that no S are P'), like the thetic denial, is a rejection; but unlike the thetic denial it involves a compound of two terms: 'He rejects Ss which are Ps'.

It would seem to be impossible to interpret the A-judgment ('He judges that all S are P') without the use of negative terms. If such terms are admitted, then we may say that the A-judgment is like the E-judgment in that it is a rejection involving a compound of two terms. It differs from the E-judgment in that one of the two terms in the compound is negative: 'He rejects Ss which are non-Ps'. We could also say 'He rejects S-which-is-non-P'. This definition presupposes that it is not possible to dispense with negative terms in Brentano's theory of judgment.

According to the traditional account, the A-judgment and the I-judgment are affirmative; the E-judgment and the O-judgment are negative; the A-judgment and the E-judgment are universal; and the I-judgment and the O-judgment are particular. But Brentano says that one judges affirmatively if one accepts something and one judges negatively if one rejects something. Hence, given this terminology, he can say that the universal judgments, A and E, are negative and the particular judgments, I and O, are affirmative.

In a discussion of Brentano's *Psychology*, J.P. N. Land had noted that normally, when we use a *sentence* of the 'Every S is P' form, our use *presupposes* the existence of Ss. [J.P.N. Land, 'On a Supposed Improvement in Formal Logic', *Proceedings of the Royal Dutch Academy*, Royal Dutch Acadamy 1876.]

Brentano conceded this point, saying that 'the ambiguity of linguistic terms is responsible for there being a multiplicity of judgments in a sentence of categorical form'[*Wahrheit und Evidenz*, p. 42]. An 'Every S is P' sentence, then, can be used to express two judgments: (a) the thetic affirmation of S, and (b) the rejection of Ss which are non-Ps.

17[a] Chr. v. Sigwart, German philosopher, 1830–1905.

17[b] A. Fick, German physiologist, 1829–1901.

17[c] Newton's discovery (through separating white light with a prism) of the phenomenon of colour mixing led Thomas Young (English physicist and physician, 1773–1829) in 1802 to postulate that there are three kinds of receptors in the eye, each one particularly sensitive to a specific part of the spectrum. Helmholtz developed this hypothesis into what is now known as the 'Young-Helmholtz tri-chromatic theory of colour vision': there are three sorts of cones in the retina, one absorbing predominantly in the red part of the spectrum, another in the green part and the third in the blue. A yellow light would thus stimulate the red and the green sensitive cones and the 'combined sensation' would be that of yellow.

The fact that there are indeed three types of cones has since been directly verified, yet in recent years another aspect of the Young-Helmholtz theory – namely its 'genetic' claim that colour sensations are determined solely by the ratio of the fluxes of the light in the three light bands (coming from the perceived object) – has come under attack for being unable to explain such phenomena as colour constancy or simultaneous contrast. One of the more recent responses to this is E. Land's 'retinex theory' of colour vision, suggesting that colour sensations depend on the lightness (determined relative to the whole 'visual scene') in each wave band. A lucid, non-technical account of this view can be found in the December issue of the *Scientific American* Vol 237, (1977) pp. 108–29.

18 Concerning Fick and Young-Helmholtz see A. Fick, '*Die Lehre von der Lichtempfindung*' in L. Hermann, *Handbuch der Physiologie*, Vol. II,

Leipzig: Vogel 1879, pp. 139–234. Fick discusses Young's theory of colour-sensation (*'Youngs Theorie der Farbempfindung'*) on pp. 194 ff.

18ª J.F. Herbart, German philosopher, pedagogue and psychologist, 1776–1841.

19 See Brentano's discussion of Kant's theory of judgment and its relation to what Kant says about the ontological argument in *Vom Dasein Gottes*, pp. 33 ff.

According to Herbart, the judgment 'some person [or another] is ill' is only hypothetical because it contains the implicit precondition 'if a person exists'. See Brentano's discussion in *Psychology from an Empirical Standpoint*, p. 214, and the notes by Kraus on the subject which appear as footnotes in that same text.

19ª F.A. Lange, German philosopher and sociologist, 1828–75.

19ᵇ Although Brentano's 'blind spot' is meant to be a phenomenal location in the visual field, I believe that with the phrase 'as there is towards the back' he can only have meant to refer to physical locations behind the observer, which have no corresponding phenomenal location in the visual field.

19ᶜ In his analysis of sounds, Helmholtz used hollow spheres as acoustic resonators (the so-called 'Helmholtz-resonators') which start to resonate if one of the frequencies associated with the sound to be analysed corresponds to their eigen-frequencies.

19ᵈ Th. Billroth, German/Austrian surgeon, 1829–94.

19ᵉ R. Koch, German bacteriologist, 1843–1910.

20 Meinong had held that it is possible for a judgment to be both evident and false. See his *'Zur erkenntnistheoretischen Würdigung des Gedächtnisses', Vierteljahresschrift für wissenschaftliche Philosophie* X (1886), pp. 7–33, reprinted in Vol. II of the *Meinong-Gesamtausgabe*, R. Kindlinger and R. Haller (eds), Graz: Akademische Druck- und Verlagsanstalt 1971, pp. 185–213. Brentano took Meinong's doctrine to be *'widersinnig'* [absurd]; see *Wahrheit und Evidenz*, p. 69.

21 Brentano here refers to one of his lectures, first published in 1874 and reprinted in *Über die Zukunft der Philosophie*, Hamburg: Meiner 1968, pp. 83–100.

21ª For an explication of the term 'di-energy' see Smith, *op. cit.* (Note 8a.) pp. 9f.

21ᵇ For an interpretation of the passage given under 41. (a) and (b) see B.

185

Müller, 'Proterosis, Proteraesthesis and Noticing a Red Tint', in *Brentano Studien*, forthcoming.

21[c] Let me give an example which illustrates my interpretation of Brentano's text: A_1: = 'John is tall'; N_1: = 'John is not tall'; A_2: = 'The apple is red'; N_2: = 'Nine is not a prime number'.

A_1 and N_1 differ *only* in quality. According to Brentano, one notices the differing qualities (i.e. affirmativeness and negativeness) simultaneously when presented with the pair A_1 and N_1, and this can, on its own, lead directly to a noticing of quality (of judgments) in general. In any case, the simultaneous noticing of the differing qualities given in A_1 and N_1 facilitates greatly the noticing of 'quality' as a general attribute (of parts) of judgments. If it isn't achieved directly, then we only need to add a further two statements like A_2 and N_2. The point in choosing them is (a) to make sure that there is some respect other than quality in which they differ (in the present case, this is achieved by a difference in matter – note: if the presentation of the first pair does not induce a noticing of quality, then we can hardly expect that the addition of a pair like A'_2 = 'The apple is red'; N'_2 = 'The apple is not red' would be of any help; and (b) to make sure that one of them has the same quality as A_1 and the other the same as N_1. Given A_1, A_2, N_1 and N_2, we are thus meant to notice immediately that (a) the way in which A_1 and A_2 differ is different from the way in which A_1 and N_1 differ; and (b) the way in which A_1 and A_2 differ is different from the way in which A_2 and N_2 differ. And this, I take it, Brentano thinks is tantamount to noticing quality in general.

21[d] J. Müller, German physiologist and pathologist, 1801–58.

21[e] Sir William Hamilton, Scottish logician and philosopher, 1788–1856.

21[f] Brentano refers here to the intuitive grasp of the purely conceptually induced conditions concerning the unification of elements.

21[g] R. Franz (originally, R.F. Knauth), German composer 1820–92.

22 See G.T. Fechner, *Elemente der Psychophysik*, 2 Parts, Leipzig 1860, here reprint, Amsterdam: Bonset 1964, Part 1, pp. 71 ff. In this text, Fechner did not use the term '*Gleichmerklichkeit*' but '*Methode der eben merklichen Unterschiede*' [method of the just noticeable differences].

For a comparison between Brentano's views and those of Fechner, of other psychologists and of contemporary psychology in general, see L. Pongratz, *Problemgeschichte der Psychologie*, Berne and Munich: Francke 1967, in particular pp. 124 ff., 136 f., 163 f.

23 For example, *Untersuchungen zur Sinnespsychologie*, pp. 176–208.

23[a] F. Suarez, Spanish theologian and philosopher, 1548–1619.

24 See also *Psychology from an Empirical Standpoint*, pp. 365 ff.

24ᵃ G.T. Fechner, German physicist, psychologist and philosopher, 1801–1887.

25 Here, Brentano probably refers to Fechner's *Elemente der Psycho-physik*, Vol. II, pp. 381 ff., in particular 392 f., where Fechner discusses the question about the 'seat of the soul'.

26 Brentano's final views on the self, on consciousness and on individuation may be found in his *Kategorienlehre*, pp. 145–65.

26ᵃ The paraphrase for 'mutually pervading' which Brentano introduces here, i.e. 'concrescent', has the same etymological root as 'concrete', namely the Latin *'concrescere'* ('to grow together'). (Note also Brentano's use of 'concreta' on p. 94.

26ᵇ H. Ebbinghaus, German psychologist, 1850–1909.

26ᶜ See also B. Müller, 'Proterosis, Proteraesthesis and Noticing a Red Tint,' in *Brentano Studien*, forthcoming.

27 Aristotle, *Problemata*, XXXV, 10, 965a, 36–40. Compare also *Sinnes-psychologie*, p. 226 where the two-finger experiment is discussed without mentioning Aristotle.

28 Saturation and colouring are discussed in *Untersuchungen zur Sinnes-psychologie*, pp. 66 f. and 215–7.

29 E.G. Boring, *The Physical Dimensions of Consciousness*, New York and London: The Century Co. 1933, p. 24.

30 Brentano's conception of intensity was quite different from that of the other psychologists of his time. Most of the others understood the term in such a way that the variations in *brightness* of a visual sensation could be identified with variations of the *intensity* of that sensation. One could then say that the intensity of a sensation is a quantity that is functionally dependent upon the external stimulus. But if difference in intensity can be noted in mere fantasy, then such differences should not be defined by reference to external stimuli. Yet we can speak of *quantities of intensity*: the intensity of one sensation can be greater than that of another. And if one thing can be said to be greater than another, in the strict sense of the term, then the second thing must be equal in a *part* to the first thing.

According to Brentano's conception of intensity, the intensity of a given quality is a function of the quantity of sensible space that is filled by that quality. If a quality becomes less intense while retaining its spatial extension, then unnoticeable portions of the visual field within the area of this extension have lost their quality. If the quality becomes more intense, then more portions of the visual field within that area have taken on that quality. And so intensity is a derived magnitude: the magnitude of intensity of a given quality is a function of the amount of space that is filled by that quality. The concept of noticing, as we have said, is essential to this theory: when a quality becomes less intense, we do not notice the places that now cease to be filled by that quality.

Intensity, then, is ascribable to the different sense-fields in the same sense and not merely in analogous senses. And in every sense-field differences of intensity are reducible to spatial differences. Hence intensity disappears as an independent category.

Brentano's theory of intensity has the consequence that the field of vision exhibits *no* degrees of intensity. (In this respect, Brentano's views are like those of E. Herting.) For there are no 'phenomenally empty places' in the field of vision (*Untersuchungen zur Sinnes-psychologie*, p. 74. The field of vision is always completely filled. If the external stimuli cease to function and the subject remains conscious, then he will at least experience the 'colour' black.

It should be emphasized that Brentano is *not* saying that visual phenomena lack intensity. He is saying, rather, that the visual field always manifests the *highest degree* of intensity. And to say this, he believes, is consistent with speaking of the relative intensities of different colours within the visual field: although any one place in the visual field has the same intensity as any other, a given place may exhibit a greater intensity of redness, say, than a certain other place. Of the colours, only grey is not thus subject to degrees of intensity.

31 Brentano discusses the inner perception of causation in his *Kategorien-lehre*, pp. 185–90.

31[a] The magnitude F_T of the tangential force of a body in uniform circular motion with (momentary rectilinear) speed v, angular speed v_a and mass m is given by the formula $F_T = m \, v_a \, v$. This means, in particular, that two uniformly circularly moving bodies with the same mass, the same angular speed and the same tangential acceleration will have the same (momentary rectilinear) speed, regardless of the radius of their motion. Thus, if we fictitiously dissolve the tie with the acting centripetal force/acceleration, we are left with two bodies which move rectilinearly with the same speed. There remains in this fiction no trace of the curvilinear natures which differentiate the two original motions. In particular, there is no trace of the difference arising from the different modes of curvature, i.e. the different curvatures of the circular trajectories.

32 Fantasy is treated in detail by Brentano in *Grundzüge der Ästhetik*, Hamburg: Meiner 1969, pp. 65–87.

32[a] G. Cantor, German mathematician, 1845–1918.

32[b] The argument Brentano is putting forward here is against Cantor's well-known theorem that the cardinality of the continuum is greater than that of the integers. Given that, today, Cantor's theorem is universally accepted within the framework of classical mathematics, how are we to judge Brentano's view? Instead of simply rejecting it, let us ask ourselves what motivated him in his claim? The text clearly shows that the issue at stake for Brentano was the sort of magnitude or 'quantity' one is to associate with continuous (and thus infinite) collections of points. And, in keeping with his later views on continuum (cf. F. Brentano, *Philosophical Investigations on Space, Time and the Continuum*, B. Smith (tr.), London: Croom Helm 1988, Part 1) his aim appears to be to discredit the atomistic conception of the continuum by showing that the associated Cantorian interpretation of magnitude as ('cardinal') *number* leads to what he considers to be an absurdity, namely a (proper) part having the same magnitude as the whole. Now, if this was indeed Brentano's intention, then the fact that the collection of points, say C, which he specifies in terms of imaginary bi-sections of some given interval I, *actually is* a proper sub-set of I (and with it Brentano's rejection of Cantor's theorem) turns out to be quite irrelevant for his argument. Why? Let us represent C as

$$C = \{ \tfrac{1}{2}, \tfrac{1}{4}, \tfrac{3}{4}, \tfrac{1}{8}, \tfrac{3}{8}, \ldots \}$$

All that is required to derive Brentano's 'absurdity' is to consider the collection

$$C' = \{ \tfrac{1}{4}, \tfrac{3}{4}, \tfrac{1}{8}, \tfrac{3}{8}, \ldots \} \text{ (i.e. } C \backslash \{ \tfrac{1}{2} \})$$

because C' (which, like C, is densely ordered, i.e. has no 'gaps' in the sense that between any two of its points there is always a third one) is clearly a proper sub-set (a 'proper part') of C, yet it has the same Cantorian magnitude as its 'whole' (i.e. C).

Being confronted with this 'absurdity', Brentano concludes that the correct solution is that, as concerns continuous manifolds, we must interpret 'magnitude' in terms of 'the specific distances of the outermost [of the] boundaries [. . .] within which the continuum [. . .] formed by them [is] situated'; a conclusion which would obviously be a vindication of his conception of continua. Yet someone of a 'classical mathematical persuasion' might well make the following objections: far from being 'absurd', the conclusion that certain collections are of equal magnitude to one of their proper parts simply amounts to the conclusion that they are infinite. The law $X \subsetneq Y \Rightarrow |X| < |Y|$ only holds for finite collections (indeed, its failure is used to define the distinctions between finite and infinite collections). Naturally, this is not meant to imply that Brentano's conception of 'magnitude' is wrong, but simply that it is by no means the only one that can be applied to continuous manifolds. After all, how else is one to interpret the fact admitted by Brentano, that a line-segment which has the magnitude of, say, four feet is nonetheless infinite.

However, having said this, a word of caution which might be used to some extent in Brentano's defence is in order: the atomistic conception of the continuum (with its embrace of actual infinities) which leads to Brentano's 'absurdity' has by no means been unchallenged in mathematical circles. Indeed, many of Brentano's views on the subject are reflected in the so-called 'intuitionist' writings of L.E.J. Brower (Dutch mathematician, 1881–1966) and H. Weyl (German mathematician, 1885–1955) [see, in particular, H. Weyl, '*Über die neue Grundlagenkrise der Mathematik*', in *Hermann Weyl: Gesammelte Abhandlungen*, K. Chandrasekrahan (ed.), Berlin: Springet, 1968, Vol. II, pp. 143–80; and '*Die heutige Erkenntnislage in der Mathematik*', ibid., pp. 511–42 (for translations of both articles see *From Brower to Hilbert: The Debate on the Foundations of Mathematics in the Twenties*, P. Mancosu (ed.), Oxford: OUP, forthcoming)].

33 On the distinction between primary and secondary continua, see *Philosophische Untersuchungen zu Raum, Zeit und Kontinuum*, pp. 28–35 (*Philosophical Investigations on Space, Time and the Continuum*, B. Smith (tr). London: Croom Helm, 1988) and *Untersuchungen zur Sinnespsychologie*, 2nd ed. pp. 198–204.

34 H. Helmholtz, *Populäre wissenschaftliche Vorträge*, 3rd journal, Braunschweig: Vieweg 1876, pp. 25 ff. Concerning Brentano's concept of a 'straight line' see 'The Brantano-Vailati Correspondence' R.M. Chisholm and M. Corrado (eds), *Topoi*, 1 (1981).

35 H. Helmholtz, *Die Tatsachen in der Wahrnehmung*, Berlin: Hirschwald 1879, pp. 8 f.: 'There are two distinct degrees of difference between sensory experiences. The deepest one is the difference between experiences which belong to different senses, such as between blue, sweet, warm [and] high pitched. I have allowed myself to refer to this as difference in the *modality* of the experiences. It is so thorough-going that it excludes any crossing over from one to the other and any relation of bigger or smaller similarity. For example, one cannot even [significantly] ask whether sweet is more similar to blue than to red. The *second, less thorough-going* kind of difference is the one between the different experiences of the same sense. I shall restrict the use of the term difference of quality to refer to it. J.G. Fichte collects these qualities of a sense in a circle of qualities, and he refers to what I have just called difference of modality as difference of the circles of quality'.

36 See *Untersuchungen zur Sinnespsychologie*, pp. 70–2, 90–2.

37 The discussion of sensation ('The General Character of Sensation') was to be followed by a 'demonstration by means of how the particular theses can be justified'. These examples involve specific questions about the psychology of sensation. Since Brentano's notes concerning these questions were very fragmentary and since most of the questions are discussed in detail in the *Untersuchungen zur Sinnespsychologie*, these notes have been omitted from the present volume.

38 Brentano is probably referring here to Hume's discussion 'Of the Infinite Divisibility of our Ideas of Space and Time', in Sections I and II of Book One of Hume's *Treatise of Human Nature*.

38ᵃ E. Mariotte, French physicist, c. 1620–64.

39 Brentano is here saying two quite different things about phenomena. One is that every phenomenon is an entity in itself, the existence of phenomena is not a particular different kind of existence. The second point is that phenomena are not *things* in themselves, for they are intentional objects and such are the insubstantial [*unwesenhafte*] correlates of certain things in themselves. Therefore, although phenomena do not have a particular kind of existence [*des Seins*], they are a particular kind of what exists [*des Seienden*].

39ᵃ Concerning the nature of experiences see also Appendix 3, in particular paragraphs 3 and 17.

40 So, for example, A. Fick in L. Hermann, *Handbuch der Psychologie*, Vol. III, Chapter 1, p. 161 and J. Sully, *Outlines of Psychology*, London: Longmans Green 1885.

40ᵃ J. Sully, British philosopher and psychologist, 1842–1923.

40ᵇ W.Th. Preyer, German psychologist and physiologist, 1841–97.

41 G.T. Fechner, *Psychophysik*, Vol. II, Leipzig: Breitkopf und Hartl 1860. On pp. 82–8 Fechner discusses the 'differentiation of difference of experiences experiences and contrast experiences'.

42 G. v. Hertling, German philosopher and Reichskanzler, cousin and pupil of Brentano, 1843–1919, *De Aristotelis notione unius*, dissertation under Trendelenburg, Berlin 1865. Concerning Brentano's influence on this dissertation, and on Hertling in general, see G. v. Hertling, *Erinnerungen aus meinem Leben*, 2 vols, Kempten: Kösel 1919/20, Vol. 1, in particular, pp. 50, 74, 161 f., 164 f.

42ᵃ E.H. Weber (German, 1795–1878) is generally considered as one of the founders of psycho-physics. In examining the differential threshold of skin and muscle sensations, Weber found that the smallest experientially appreciable difference between two stimuli ('just-noticeable difference', 'Weber fraction') of the same type is a constant fraction of these stimuli. Fechner, assuming that such smallest discernible increments in the intensity of sensation constitute equal units of sensation, derived the formula

$$S = K \log I + C,$$

where the intensity of sensation (S) is a linear function of the logarithm of the intensity of the stimulus (I) – K and C being constants. The problem with Fechner's derivation was mainly seen in the fact that the intensity of sensation cannot easily be physically measured. What has been shown since is that – over a range of stimulus intensities – the frequency of the messages from the stimulated receptor is a linear function of the stimulus intensity. Fechner's equation (thus interpreted) hence appears to describe a fundamental characteristic of sense organs. (For a detailed Bibliography of Weber's work see: *Dictionary of Scientific Biography*, Vol. XIV, New York: Scribner 1970.)

43 See, for example, *Versuch über die Erkenntnis*, Hamburg: Meiner 1970, pp 7–45, 154 f.

44 In Brentano's *Nachlass* there are two manuscripts '*Von der Zahl*', each from 1901; they are numbered Meg 2a and Meg 2b. A third, probably also from 1901, numbered Meg 2, is entitled '*Von der Zahl und dem analytischen Character der algebraischen Wahrheiten*'.

45 Compare *Vom Ursprung sittlicher Erkenntnis*, Hamburg: Meiner 1969, p. 19 and *Grundlegung und Aufbau der Ethik*, Bern: Franke 1952, pp. 144, 146 f.

46 Colour-blindness, named after the English physicist J. Dalton who described this illness in himself.

47 Brentano here maintains that intentional relations are not 'relations in the proper sense, he also defended this view in the *Klassifikation der psychischen Phänomene*, 1911, reprinted in *Psychology from an Empirical Standpoint*, see pp. 271–81 [*Psychologie vom empirischen Standpunkt*, Vol. II, pp. 133–8]. But subsequently (1915) he defends the view that intentional relations are paradigmatic cases of relations and are therefore relations in the proper sense: see *Kategorienlehre*, pp. 166–76.

INDEX

25873428R00123

Made in the USA
Lexington, KY
07 September 2013